The Poetry of Horses

The Poetry

illustrated by Ruth Sanderson

of Horses

compiled by William Cole

CHARLES SCRIBNER'S SONS   *New York*

Copyright © 1979 William Cole

Library of Congress Cataloging in Publication Data
Main entry under title:
The Poetry of horses.
Includes index.
SUMMARY: A poetry collection depicting aspects of
horses and horsemanship.
1. Horses—Juvenile poetry.   2. Children's poetry,
American.   3. Children's poetry, English.   [1. Horses—
Poetry.   2. American poetry—Collections.   3. English
poetry—Collections]   I. Cole, William, 1919–
PS595.H67P6   821'.008'036   79-9228
ISBN 0-684-16330-6

Printed in the United States of America

1 3 5 7 9 11 13 15 17 19 V/C 20 18 16 14 12 10 8 6 4 2

BT 895/828-4/80

*J 821.008
Poetry*

ACKNOWLEDGMENTS

The compiler and the publishers gratefully acknowledge the following poets, publishers, and agents for permission to reprint poems in this anthology. Every effort has been made to locate all persons having any rights or interests in the material published here. If some acknowledgments have not been made, their omission is unintentional and is regretted.

"Indecision Means Flexibility" by Elliot Abhau. By permission of the author.

"The Mare" by Herbert Asquith. From *Pillicock Hill* by Herbert Asquith, published by Macmillan Publishing Co., Inc., New York (1926) and William Heinemann Ltd. Publishers, London.

"A Mare" by Kate Barnes. Reprinted by permission; © 1959 The New Yorker Magazine, Inc.

"Lord Epsom" and "Jack and His Pony, Tom" by Hilaire Belloc. From *Cautionary Verses*, by Hilaire Belloc. Copyright 1931 and renewed 1959 by Eleanor Jebb Belloc, Elizabeth Belloc and Hilary Belloc. Reprinted by permission of Alfred A. Knopf, Inc. and Gerald Duckworth & Co., Ltd.

"Horse" by Gerard Benson. By permission of the author.

"Hunter Trials" by John Betjeman. From *Collected Poems* by John Betjeman. Reprinted by permission of John Murray (Publishers) Ltd. and Houghton Mifflin Co.

"Horse" by Randy Blasing. From *Light Years* by Randy Blasing. Copyright © 1977 by Randy Blasing. Reprinted by permission of Persea Books, Inc., 225 Lafayette Street, New York, N.Y. 10012.

"Two at Showtime" and "Morgans in October" by Suzanne Brabant. By permission of the author.

Contents

Foals
and
Colts

FOAL

Come trotting up
Beside your mother,
Little skinny.

Lay your neck across
Her back, and whinny,
Little foal.

You think you're a horse
Because you can trot—
But you're not.

Your eyes are so wild,
And each leg is as tall
As a pole;

And you're only a skittish
Child, after all,
Little foal.

MARY BRITTON MILLER

THE NEWBORN COLT

It dances—
The muscles slipping freely
Beneath the fine skin,
The small joints miracles of perfection.
In confident awareness,
In the pride of being alive,
It lifts with grace the pointed white hooves.
Between the foal and its mother is a great love.
It moves with her almost as one,
Yet in no way bound,
While every upright shining hair
On its short ruffle of a mane,
Dances with joy.

MARY KENNEDY

BIRTH OF THE FOAL

As May was opening the rosebuds,
elder and lilac beginning to bloom,
it was time for the mare to foal.
She'd rest herself, or hobble lazily

after the boy who sang as he led her
to pasture, wading through the meadowflowers.

They wandered back at dusk, bone-tired,
the moon perched on a blue shoulder of sky.

Then the mare lay down,
sweating and trembling, on her straw in the stable.
The drowsy, heavy-bellied cows
surrounded her, waiting, watching, snuffing.

Later, when even the hay slept
and the shaft of the Plow pointed south,
the foal was born. Hours the mare
spent licking the foal with its glue-blind eyes.

And the foal slept at her side,
a heap of feathers ripped from a bed.
Straw never spread as soft as this.
Milk or snow never slept like a foal.

Dawn bounced up in a bright red hat,
waved at the world and skipped away.
Up staggered the foal,
its hooves were jelly-knots of foam.

Then day sniffed with its blue nose
through the open stable window, and found them—
the foal nuzzling its mother,
velvet fumbling for her milk.

Then all the trees were talking at once,
chickens scrabbled in the yard,

like golden flowers
envy withered the last stars.

FERENC JUHÁSZ

*(translated from the
Hungarian by David Wevill)*

HORSE

All
fall it stuck
close to it's mother's snow-
capped ass. How
gingerly it
nibbled at
the grass, as if its legs
were too long
for its neck, as
though it were
floating just
off the ground . . .

              A

yearling this
March, it stands apart
from its mother. Now
it sticks its

neck out &
tests its legs, as though
it were walking
on air, as if, by
grace made
weightless, it
could fly.

RANDY BLASING

UNCLAIMED

You can go in the stall. It's a mare and her first colt,
A palomino, a nice little thing
Too weak to fight for his natural food and bring
The milk down that the mare holds back. The men
Brought them in separately. The colt was found
In a neighbour's pasture; he must have rolled around
Or been pushed under a fence. Nothing like that
Ever happened before that I know of. Now the mare
Thinks that it's not her colt. We don't dare
Leave them alone. She's hobbled. She'd kick him sure.
You can't blame her, either. We'll have to take
Her back to the pasture. Somebody will have to make
That colt feed on a bottle every two hours.
Yes, they're heating milk now in the kitchen. It's too bad
That's about the best-looking colt we ever had.

FLORIDA WATTS SMYTH

FOR A SHETLAND PONY BROOD MARE
WHO DIED IN HER BARREN YEAR

After bringing forth eighteen
foals in as many Mays
you might, old Trinket girl,
have let yourself be lulled
this spring into the green days
of pasture and first curl
of timothy. Instead,
your milk bag swelled again,
an obstinate machine.
Your long pale tongue
waggled in every feed box.
You slicked your ears back
to scatter other mares
from the salt lick.
You were full of winter burdocks
and false pregnancy.

By midsummer all the foals
had breached, except the ghost
you carried. In the bog
where you came down each noon
to ease your deer-thin hoofs in mud,
a jack-in-the-pulpit cocked
his overhang like a question mark.
We saw some autumn soon
that botflies would take your skin
and bloodworms settle
inside the cords and bands

that laced your belly,
your church of folded hands.
But all in good time, Trinket!
Was it something you understood?
Full of false pride
you lay down and died
in the sun,
all silken on one side,
all mud on the other one.

MAXINE KUMIN

Beginners

INDECISION MEANS FLEXIBILITY

A foot in the stirrup,
one foot on the ground,
no wish to mount up and
afraid to get down,
I'm wondering how long
"Old Dobbin" will wait
for this headless horseman
to take hold of his fate.

ELLIOT ABHAU

RIDING

I learned to ride with the Colonel
a Russian with an interesting past.

My shiny boots
my ponytail tucked beneath my hat
I was skinny and twelve.

Indoors
a large corral
I learned to mount—
the quick shove
the flight over the top.

I gasped at how high I sat
the intricacy of the reins
through my fingers.

I travelled the ring
circling crossing
he in the center commanded
cracking his crop against his boot.
I learned to post
the posture the grace
a dime between my knee and the horse
the easy leap of a canter.

Outdoors
a narrow trail
I rode beside the Colonel
stirrup to stirrup.

One day you will ride like this
with a young man, he said.
I never brought the horse back in a sweat.
I kept the pace.

Only later I learned
It was not my hands on the reins
the horse had obeyed
but his voice.

FLORENCE GROSSMAN

LEARNER

I thought a horse was "Gee!" and "Whoa!"
　　Four legs, a head and a mane;
But it's worse than algebra, he has so
　　Befuddled my poor young brain.

Forelock and fetlock, which is which?
　　Do stevedores line his dock?
Is his nose his nozzle, or just a snitch?
　　His *muzzle?* And where's his hock?

I can show you his tail, I can point to his jaw,
　　I'm not such a nincompoop;
But—ergot and cannon, chestnut and haw,
　　Poll, gaskin, withers and croup,

Pastern and atlas, stifle and sheath,
　　Brisket and coronet—
Are they round at the back? On top? Underneath?
　　When they tell me, I just forget.

I've groomed him well, and he looks superb—
　　So do I in my smart new gear;
But—neckstrap, noseband, pommel and curb,
　　Cavesson—dear, oh dear!

Snaffle and numnah, roller and girth,
　　Surcingle round his tum—
I may be the puzzledest girl on earth,
　　But—Pony Club, here I come!

J. A. LINDON

NEW SKILLS

I am learning how to make a horse go left.
We are sitting in the middle of a field.
Actually the horse is standing
And I am sitting on top of the horse.
I am kicking the horse, tapping my heels
On its flanks, tugging the reins.
The horse is snorting through its nostrils.
Small bubbles of rebellion appear on the nose.
The horse does not want to go left.
For a long time now the horse has been wanting to go
    right.
I have tried not to let him.
We came from the right
And I am not yet ready to go home.

NAOMI SHIHAB NYE

THE CENTAUR

The summer that I was ten—
Can it be there was only one
summer that I was ten? It must

have been a long one then—
each day I'd go out to choose
a fresh horse from my stable

which was a willow grove
down by the old canal.
I'd go on my two bare feet.

But when, with my brother's jack-knife,
I had cut me a long limber horse
with a good thick knob for a head,

and peeled him slick and clean
except a few leaves for the tail,
and cinched my brother's belt

around his head for a rein.
I'd straddle and canter him fast
up the grass bank to the path,

trot along in the lovely dust
that talcumed over his hoofs,
hiding my toes, and turning

his feet to swift half-moons.
The willow knob with the strap
bouncing between my thighs

was the pommel and yet the poll
of my nickering pony's head.
My head and my neck were mine,

yet they were shaped like a horse.
My hair flopped to the side
like the mane of a horse in the wind.

My forelock swung in my eyes,
my neck arched and I snorted.
I shied and skittered and reared,

stopped and raised my knees,
pawed at the ground and quivered.
My teeth bared as we wheeled

and swished through the dust again.
I was the horse and the rider,
and the leather I slapped to his rump

spanked my own behind.
Doubled, my two hoofs beat
a gallop along the bank.

The wind twanged in my mane,
my mouth squared to the bit.
And yet I sat on my steed

quiet, negligent riding,
my toes standing the stirrups,
my thighs hugging his ribs.

At a walk we drew up to the porch.
I tethered him to a paling.
Dismounting, I smoothed my skirt

and entered the dusky hall.
My feet on the clean linoleum
left ghostly toes in the hall.

Where have you been? said my mother.
Been riding, I said from the sink
and filled me a glass of water.

What's that in your pocket? she said.
Just my knife. It weighted my pocket
and stretched my dress awry.

Go tie back your hair, said my mother,
and *Why is your mouth all green?*
*Rob Roy, he pulled some clover
as we crossed the field,* I told her.

MAY SWENSON

RIDING LESSON

I learned two things
from an early riding teacher.
He held a nervous filly
in one hand and gestured
with the other, saying, "Listen.
Keep one leg on one side,
the other leg on the other side,
and your mind in the middle."

He turned and mounted.
She took two steps, then left

the ground, I thought for good.
But she came down hard, humped
her back, swallowed her neck,
and threw her rider as you'd
throw a rock. He rose, brushed
his pants and caught his breath,
and said, "See, that's the way
to do it. When you see
they're gonna throw you, get off."

HENRY TAYLOR

FLYING CHANGES

First time I ever saw a flying change,
Frisbee did it, but I didn't know what
I was watching.
He cantered in a circle, white neck arched.
A kind of twinkling skip of his front legs,
And slick as paint, he curved the other way.

Perched high on top the paddock rail,
I envied so the girl up on his back,
So coolly showing off his gaits—
And all those ribbons she'd won with him.
(Mom told me later that she pitied her. It's only now that
    I know what she meant.)

A pony's what I'd dreamed of for so long,
I couldn't breathe for fear the price would be,
A whole lot higher than we'd want to pay.

Never thought I'd learn the flying change,
Yet finally I did, but not before
I'd fumbled through a lot of other things,
Like how to tack him up, rise to the trot,
Sit cantering, pick hooves, shine boots, muck stalls.
I finally even learned to bring him slow
Into his fences on an outside course.
Then, just like that, I began to grow.

Still hate that tweedy friend of Mom's.
She yelled it at the schooling show, last spring,
"You realize, don't you, that your son, looks all out of
    proportion on that pony?"
Began to feel my boots would scrape the ground,
Shortening the stirrups didn't help for long.
I kept on growing, changing every day.
He stayed the same, fourteen three hands, my friend.
Fourteen years old, exact same age as me.

At first I thought I'd keep him as a pet.
Out in the field, to play with, rub his nose,
But then I thought it wasn't fair to let
An athlete like him get soft and fat.
Not fair to him, nor to some other kid,
And so we ran an ad.

One day she came, a skinny little thing,
With braces on her teeth and two pigtails.

I knew right off that she would be the one.
She stood all eyes, as I pulled tight his girth,
And feeling old, began the warming up,
Around the ring at walk, then trot, canter.
Frisbee and I performed the flying change.

MARY WOOD

Horse
Tales

WIDDECOMBE FAIR

"Tom Pearse, Tom Pearse, lend me your gray mare,
All along, down along, out along, lee.
For I want for to go to Widdecombe Fair,
Wi' Bill Brewer, Jan Stewer, Peter Gurney, Peter
Davy, Dan'l Whiddon, Harry Hawk,
Old Uncle Tom Cobley and all."
Old Uncle Tom Cobley and all.

"And when shall I see again my gray mare?"
All along, down along, out along, lee.
"By Friday soon, or Saturday noon,
Wi' Bill Brewer, Jan Stewer, Peter Gurney, Peter
Davy, Dan'l Whiddon, Harry Hawk,
Old Uncle Tom Cobley and all."
Old Uncle Tom Cobley and all.

Then Friday came and Saturday noon,
All along, down along, out along, lee.
But Tom Pearse's old mare hath not trotted home,
Wi' Bill Brewer, Jan Stewer, Peter Gurney, Peter
Davy, Dan'l Whiddon, Harry Hawk,
Old Uncle Tom Cobley and all.
Old Uncle Tom Cobley and all.

So Tom Pearse he got up to the top o' the hill,
All along, down along, out along, lee.
And he seed his old mare down a-making her will,
Wi' Bill Brewer, Jan Stewer, Peter Gurney, Peter
Davy, Dan'l Whiddon, Harry Hawk,

Old Uncle Tom Cobley and all.
Old Uncle Tom Cobley and all.

So Tom Pearse's old mare her took sick and her died,
All along, down along, out along, lee.
And Tom he sat down on a stone, and he cried
Wi' Bill Brewer, Jan Stewer, Peter Gurney, Peter
Davy, Dan'l Whiddon, Harry Hawk,
Old Uncle Tom Cobley and all.
Old Uncle Tom Cobley and all.

But this isn't the end o' this shocking affair,
All along, down along, out along, lee.
Nor, though they be dead, of the horrid career
Of Bill Brewer, Jan Stewer, Peter Gurney, Peter
Davy, Dan'l Whiddon, Harry Hawk,
Old Uncle Tom Cobley and all.
Old Uncle Tom Cobley and all.

When the wind whistles cold on the moor of a night,
All along, down along, out along, lee.
Tom Pearse's old mare doth appear, gashly white,
Wi' Bill Brewer, Jan Stewer, Peter Gurney, Peter
Davy, Dan'l Whiddon, Harry Hawk,
Old Uncle Tom Cobley and all.
Old Uncle Tom Cobley and all.

And all the long night he heard skirling and groans,
All along, down along, out along, lee.
From Tom Pearse's old mare in her rattling bones,
And from Bill Brewer, Jan Stewer, Peter Gurney,
Peter Davy, Dan'l Whiddon, Harry Hawk,

Old Uncle Tom Cobley and all.
Old Uncle Tom Cobley and all.

(OLD ENGLISH SONG)

THE ZEBRA DUN

We were camped on the plains at the head of the
Cimarron
When along came a stranger and stopped to arger some,
He seemed so very foolish that we began to look around,
We thought he was a greenhorn that had just 'scaped
from town.

We asked if he'd been to breakfast; he hadn't had a
smear,
So we opened up the chuck-box and bade him have his
share.
He took a cup of coffee and some biscuits and some
beans,
And then began to talk and tell about foreign kings and
queens—

About the Spanish war and the fighting on the seas
With guns as big as steers and ramrods big as trees—
And about Old Paul Jones, a mean, fighting son of a
gun,
Who was the grittiest cuss that ever pulled a gun.

Such an educated feller, his thoughts just came in herds,
He astonished all them cowboys with them jaw-breaking
     words.
He just kept on talking till he made the boys all sick,
And they began to look around just how to play a trick.

He said that he had lost his job upon the Santa Fe
And was going across the plains to strike the 7-D.
He didn't say how come it, some trouble with the boss,
But said he'd like to borrow a nice fat saddle hoss.

This tickled all the boys to death, they laughed down in
     their sleeves—
"We'll lend you a horse just as fresh and fat as you
     please."
Shorty grabbed a lariat and roped the Zebra Dun,
Turned him over to the stranger and waited for the fun.

Old Dunny was a rocky outlaw that had grown so awful
     wild
That he could paw the white out of the moon every jump
     for a mile.
Old Dunny stood right still—as if he didn't know—
Until he was saddled and ready for to go.

When the stranger hit the saddle, old Dunny quit the
     earth
And traveled right straight up for all that he was worth.
A-pitching and a-squealing, a-having walleyed fits,
His hind feet perpendicular, his front ones in the bits.

We could see the tops of the mountains under Dunny
    every jump,
But the stranger he was growed there just like the
    camel's hump;
The stranger sat upon him and curled his black mustache
Just like a summer boarder waiting for his hash.

He thumped him in the shoulders and spurred him
    when he whirled,
To show them flunky punchers that he was the wolf of
    the world.
When the stranger had dismounted once more upon the
    ground,
We knew he was a thoroughbred and not a gent from
    town.

The boss who was standing round, a-watching of the
    show,
Walked right up to the stranger and told him he needn't
    go—
"If you can use the lasso like you rode old Zebra Dun,
You're the man I've been looking for ever since the year
    of one."

Oh, he could twirl the lariat and he didn't do it slow,
He could catch them forefeet nine out of ten for any kind
    of dough.
And when the herd stampeded he was always on the
    spot
And set them to nothing, like the boiling of a pot.

There's one thing and a shore thing I've learned since
  I've been born,
That every educated feller ain't a plumb greenhorn.

(AMERICAN COWBOY BALLAD)

THE GLORY TRAIL

'Way high up the Mogollons,
    Among the mountaintops,
A lion cleaned a yearlin's bones
    And licked his thankful chops,
When on the picture who should ride,
    A-trippin' down a slope,
But High-Chin Bob, with sinful pride
    And mav'rick-hungry rope.

    "Oh, glory be to me," says he,
      "And fame's unfadin' flowers!
    All meddlin' hands are far away;
    I ride my good top-hawse today
    And I'm top-rope of the Lazy J—
      Hi! kitty cut, you're ours!"

That lion licked his paw so brown
    And dreamed soft dreams of veal—
And then the circlin' loop sung down
    And roped him 'round his meal.

He yowled quick fury to the world
    Till all the hills yelled back;
The top-hawse gave a snort and whirled
    And Bob caught up the slack.

    "Oh, glory be to me," laughs he.
      "We've hit the glory trail.
    No human man as I have read
    Darst loop a ragin' lion's head,
    Nor ever hawse could drag one dead
      Until we told the tale."

'Way high up the Mogollons
    That top-hawse done his best,
Through whippin' brush and rattlin' stones,
    From canyon-floor to crest.
But ever when Bob turned and hoped
    A limp remains to find,
A red-eyed lion, belly roped
    But healthy, loped behind.

    "Oh, glory be to me," grunts he.
      "This glory trail is rough,
    Yet even till the Judgment Morn
    I'll keep this dally 'round the horn,
    For never any hero born
      Could stoop to holler: 'Nuff!' "

Three suns had rode their circle home
    Beyond the desert's rim,
And turned their star-herds loose to roam
    The ranges high and dim;

Yet up and down and 'round and 'cross
    Bob pounded, weak and wan,
For pride still glued him to his hawse
    And glory drove him on.

"Oh, glory be to me," sighs he.
    "He kaint be drug to death,
But now I know beyond a doubt
Them heroes I have read about
Was only fools that stuck it out
    To end of mortal breath."

'Way high up the Mogollons
    A prospect man did swear
That moon dramas melted down his bones
    And hoisted up his hair:
A ribby cow-hawse thundered by,
    A lion trailed along,
A rider, ga'nt but chin on high,
    Yelled out a crazy song.

"Oh, glory be to me!" cries he,
    "And to my noble noose!
Oh, stranger, tell my pards below
I took a rampin' dream in tow,
And if I never lay him low,
    I'll never turn him loose!"

BADGER CLARK

32

DANIEL WEBSTER'S HORSES

If when the wind blows
Rattling the trees
Clicking like skeletons'
Elbows and knees,

You hear along the road
Three horses pass—
Do not go near the dark
Cold window glass.

If when the first snow lies
Whiter than bones
You see the mark of hoofs
Cut to the stones,

Hoofs of three horses
Going abreast—
Turn about, turn about,
A closed door is best!

Upright in the earth
Under the sod
They buried three horses
Bridled and shod,

Daniel Webster's horses—
He said as he grew old,
"Flesh, I loved riding,
Shall I not love it, cold?

"Shall I not love to ride
Bone astride bone,
When the cold wind blows
And snow covers stone?

"Bury them on their feet
With bridle and bit.
They were fine horses—
See their shoes fit."

ELIZABETH COATSWORTH

RAIN-IN-THE-FACE

The rain falls in my face
because I look up
for the sun.
"Watch out,"
people call to me,
"you're going to trip."

But every night now
for a month
I have run away
to the blue lake
where the wild horses
come to drink.

I talk to my clumsy hands.
I scold my feet.
I hide
and watch the horses,
calling their names softly,
names I invent.

"Here, Thunder Cloud!
Here, Swan Neck!"
The first time they run.
The second, they snort
and drink quickly,
twitching their ears.

Now they stiffen there,
tails high and rigid,
and they look at me.
Then they drink a long time
and lift their necks
and look again.

In the moonlight
the white coats are blue
and the bays are shadows.
I stand perfectly still.
My legs grow long and powerful.
I will run with the horses.

My hands hold the branches apart
as I stand in the bushes.
I take a step or two forward,
my skin silky and quivering.

"Here, Friends,
don't be afraid."

No wonder I am tired
all the next day.

MARY CROW

HOW WE DROVE THE TROTTER

Oh, he was a handsome trotter, and he couldn't be
    completer,
He had such a splendid action and he trotted to this
    metre,
Such a pace and such a courage, such a record-killing
    power,
That he did his mile in two-fifteen, his twenty in the
    hour.
When he trotted on the Bathurst road the pace it was a
    panter,
But he broke the poet's rhythm when he broke out in a
    canter—

As we were remarking the pace was a panter,
But just as we liked it he broke in a canter,
And rattled along with a motion terrific,
And scattered the sparks with a freedom prolific;

He tugged at the bit and he jerked at the bridle,
We pulled like a demon, the effort was idle,
The bit in his teeth and the rein in the crupper,
We didn't much care to get home to our supper.

            Then we went
            Like the wind,
            And our hands
            They were skinned,
            And we thought
            With a dread
            To go over his head,
            And we tugged
            And we strove,
            Couldn't say
            That we drove
            Till we found
            It had stopped
            And the gallop was dropped!

Then he dropped into a trot again as steady as a pacer,
And we thought we had a dandy that was sure to make a
      racer
That would rival all the Yankees and was bound to beat
      the British,
Not a bit of vice about him though he was a trifle
      skittish;
Past the buggies and the sulkies on the road we went a-
      flying,
For the pace it was a clinker, and they had no chance of
      trying,

But for fear he'd start a canter we were going to stop his
    caper
When he bolted like a bullet at a flying piece of paper—

      Helter skelter,
      What a pelter!
      Such a pace to win a welter!
        Rush,
        Race,
        Tear!
       Flying through the air!
      Wind a-humming,
      Fears benumbing,
      Here's another trap a-coming!
        Shouts!
        Bash!
        Crash!
      Moses, what a smash!

W. T. GOODGE

THE PONIES

During the strike, the ponies were brought up
From their snug stables, some three hundred feet
Below the surface—up the pit's main shaft
Shot one by one into the light of day;

And as each stepped, bewildered, from the cage,
He stood among his fellows, shivering
In the unaccustomed freshness of free air,
His dim eyes dazzled by the April light.
And then one suddenly left the huddle group,
Lifted his muzzle, sniffed the freshness in,
Pawed the soft turf and, whinneying, started trotting
Across the field; and one by one his fellows
With pricking ears each slowly followed him,
Timidly trotting: when the leader's trot
Broke into a canter, then into a gallop;
And now the whole herd galloped at his heels
Around the dewy meadow, hard hoofs, used
To stumbling over treacherous stony tramways
And plunging hock-deep through black steamy puddles
Of the dusky narrow galleries, delighting
In the soft spring of the resilient turf.
Still round and round the field they raced, unchecked
By tugging traces, at their heels no longer
The trundling tubs, and round and round and round,
With a soft thunder of hoofs, the sunshine flashing
On their sleek coats, through the bright April weather
They raced all day; and even when the night
Kindled clear stars above them in a sky
Strangely unsullied by the stack which now
No longer belched out blackness, still they raced,
Unwearied, as through their short sturdy limbs
The rebel blood like wildfire ran, their lungs
Filled with the breath of freedom. On they sped
Through the sweet dewy darkness; and all night
The watchman at the pithead heard the thudding
Of those careering and exultant hoofs

Still circling in a crazy chase; and dawn
Found them still streaming raggedly around,
Tailing into a lagging cantering,
And so to a stumbling trot: when gradually,
Dropping out one by one, they started cropping
The dew-dank tender grass, which no foul reek
From the long idle pit now smirched, and drinking
With quivering nostrils the rich living breath
Of sappy growing things, the cool rank green
Grateful to eyes, familiar from their colthood
Only with darkness and the dusty glimmer
Of lamplit galleries . . .
Mayhap one day
Our masters, too, will go on strike, and we
Escape the dark and drudgery of the pit,
And race unreined around the fields of heaven!

WILFRID GIBSON

GROG-AN'-GRUMBLE STEEPLECHASE

'Twixt the coastline and the border lay the town of Grog-
     an'-Grumble
     (Just two pubs beside a racecourse in a wilderness
     of sludge)
An' they say the local meeting was a drunken rough-
     an'-tumble,

Which was ended pretty often by an inquest on the
   judge.
Yes, 'tis said the city talent very often caught a tartar
   In the Grog-an'-Grumble sportsman, 'n' retired
   with broken heads,
For the fortune, life, and safety of the Grog-an'-Grumble
   starter
   Mostly hung upon the finish of the local
   thoroughbreds.

Pat M'Durmer was the owner of a horse they called The
   Screamer,
   Which he called the "quickest shtepper 'twixt the
   Darling and the sea,"
But I think it's very doubtful if a Banshee-haunted
   dreamer
   Ever saw a more outrageous piece of equine
   scenery;
For his points were most decided, from his end to his
   beginning;
   He had eyes of different colour, and his legs they
   wasn't mates.
Pat M'Durmer said he always came "widin a flip av
   winnin',"
   An' his sire had come from England, 'n' his dam
   was from the States.

Friends would argue with M'Durmer, and they said he
   was in error
   To put up his horse The Screamer, for he'd lose in
   any case,

41

And they said a city racer by the name of Holy Terror
    Was regarded as the winner of the coming
      steeplechase;
Pat declared he had the knowledge to come in when it
    was raining,
    And irrelevantly mentioned that he knew the time
    of day,
So he rose in their opinion. It was noticed that the
    training
    Of The Screamer was conducted in a dark,
    mysterious way.

Well, the day arrived in glory; 'twas a day of jubilation
    For the careless-hearted bushmen quite a hundred
    miles around,
An' the rum 'n' beer 'n' whisky came in wagons from the
    station,
    An' the Holy Terror talent were the first upon the
    ground.
Judge M'Ard—with whose opinion it was scarcely safe to
    wrestle—
    Took his dangerous position on the bark-an'-
    sapling stand:
He was what the local Stiggins used to speak of as a
    "wessel
    Of wrath," and he'd a bludgeon that he carried in
    his hand.

"Off ye go!" the starter shouted, as down fell a stupid
    jockey;
    Off they started in disorder—left the jockey where
    he lay—

And they fell and rolled and galloped down the crooked
	course and rocky,
		Till the pumping of The Screamer could be heard a
		mile away.
But he kept his legs and galloped; he was used to rugged
	courses,
		And he lumbered down the gully till the ridge
		began to quake:
And he ploughed along the sidling, raising earth till
	other horses
		An' their riders, too, were blinded by the dust-
		cloud in his wake.

From the ruck he'd struggle slowly—they were much
	surprised to find him
		Close abeam of Holy Terror as along the flat they
		tore—
Even higher still and denser rose the cloud of dust
	behind him,
		While in more divided splinters flew the shattered
		rails before.
"Terror!" "Dead heat!" they were shouting—"Terror!"
	but The Screamer hung out
		Nose to nose with Holy Terror as across the creek
		they swung,
An' M'Durmer shouted loudly, "Put yer tongue out, put
	yer tongue out!"
		An' The Screamer put his tongue out, and he won
		by half-a-tongue.

HENRY LAWSON

THE BRONCHO THAT WOULD
NOT BE BROKEN

A little colt—broncho, loaned to the farm
To be broken in time without fury or harm,
Yet black crows flew past you, shouting alarm,
Calling "Beware," with lugubrious singing . . .
The butterflies there in the bush were romancing,
The smell of the grass caught your soul in a trance,
So why be a-fearing the spurs and the traces,
O broncho that would not be broken of dancing?

You were born with the pride of the lords great and
        olden
Who danced, through the ages, in corridors golden.
In all the wide farm-place the person most human.
You spoke out so plainly with squealing and capering,
With whinnying, snorting contorting and prancing,
And you dodged your pursuers, looking askance,
With Greek-footed figures, and Parthenon paces,
O broncho that would not be broken of dancing.

The grasshoppers cheered. "Keep whirling," they said.
The insolent sparrows called from the shed
"If men will not laugh, make them wish they were
        dead."
But arch were your thoughts, all malice displacing,
Though the horse-killers came, with snake-whips
        advancing.
You bantered and cantered away your last chance.

And they scourged you, with Hell in their speech and
        their faces.
O broncho that would not be broken of dancing.

"Nobody cares for you," rattled the crows,
As you dragged the whole reaper, next day, down the
        rows.
The three mules held back, yet you danced on your toes.
You pulled like a racer, and kept the mules chasing.
You tangled the harness with bright eyes side-glancing,
While the drunk driver bled you—a pole for a lance—
And the giant mules bit at you—keeping their places,
O broncho that would not be broken of dancing.

In that last afternoon your boyish heart broke.
The hot wind came down like a sledge-hammer stroke.
The blood-sucking flies to a rare feast awoke.
And they searched out your wounds, your death-warrant
        tracing.
And the merciful men, their religion enhancing,
Stopped the red reaper, to give you a chance.
Then you died on the prairie, and scorned all disgraces,
O broncho that would not be broken of dancing.

VACHEL LINDSAY

THE MAN FROM SNOWY RIVER

There was movement at the station, for the word had
    passed around
That the colt from old Regret had got away,
And had joined the wild bush horses—he was worth a
    thousand pound,
So all the cracks had gathered to the fray.
All the tried and noted riders from the stations near and
    far
Had mustered at the homestead overnight,
For the bushmen love hard riding where the wild bush
    horses are,
And the stock-horse snuffs the battle with delight.

There was Harrison, who made his pile when Pardon
    won the cup,
The old man with his hair as white as snow;
But few could ride beside him when his blood was fairly
    up—
He would go wherever horse and man could go.
And Clancy of the Overflow came down to lend a hand,
No better horseman ever held the reins;
For never horse could throw him while the saddle-girths
    would stand—
He learnt to ride while droving on the plains.

And one was there, a stripling on a small and weedy
    beast;
He was something like a racehorse undersized,
With a touch of Timor pony—three parts thoroughbred
    at least—

And such as are by mountain horsemen prized.
He was hard and tough and wiry—just the sort that
    won't say die—
There was courage in his quick impatient tread;
And he bore the badge of gameness in his bright and
    fiery eye,
And the proud and lofty carriage of his head.

But still so slight and weedy, one would doubt his power
    to stay,
And the old man said, "That horse will never do
For a long and tiring gallop—lad, you'd better stop
    away,
Those hills are far too rough for such as you."
So he waited, sad and wistful—only Clancy stood his
    friend—
"I think we ought to let him come," he said;
"I warrant he'll be with us when he's wanted at the end,
For both his horse and he are mountain bred.

"He hails from Snowy River, up by Kosciusko's side,
Where the hills are twice as steep and twice as rough;
Where a horse's hoofs strike firelight from the flint-
    stones every stride,
The man that holds his own is good enough.
And the Snowy River riders on the mountains make
    their home,
Where the river runs those giant hills between;
I have seen full many a horseman since I first
    commenced to roam,
But nowhere yet such horsemen have I seen."

So he went; they found the horses by the big mimosa
    clump,
They raced away towards the mountain's brow,
And the old man gave his orders, "Boys, go at them from
    the jump,
No use to try for fancy riding now.
And, Clancy, you must wheel them, try and wheel them
    to the right.
Ride boldly, lad, and never fear the spills,
For never yet was rider that could keep the mob in sight,
If once they gain the shelter of those hills."

So Clancy rode to wheel them—he was racing on the
    wing
Where the best and boldest riders take their place,
And he raced his stock-horse past them, and he made
    the ranges ring
With the stockwhip, as he met them face to face.
Then they halted for a moment, while he swung the
    dreaded lash,
But they saw their well-loved mountain full in view,
And they charged beneath the stockwhip with a sharp
    and sudden dash,
And off into the mountain scrub they flew.

Then fast the horsemen followed, where the gorges deep
    and black
Resounded to the thunder of their tread,
And the stockwhips woke the echoes, and they fiercely
    answered back
From cliffs and crags that beetled overhead.

And upward, ever upward, the wild horses held their
        way,
Where mountain ash and kurrajong grew wide;
And the old man muttered fiercely, "We may bid the
        mob good-day,
No man can hold them down the other side."

When they reached the mountain's summit, even Clancy
        took a pull—
It well might make the boldest hold their breath;
The wild hop scrub grew thickly, and the hidden ground
        was full
Of wombat holes, and any slip was death.
But the man from Snowy River let the pony have his
        head,
And he swung his stockwhip round and gave a cheer,
And he raced him down the mountain like a torrent
        down its bed
While the others stood and watched in very fear.

He sent the flint-stones flying, but the pony kept his
        feet,
He cleared the fallen timber in his stride,
And the man from Snowy River never shifted in his
        seat—
It was grand to see that mountain horseman ride.
Through the stringybarks and saplings, on the rough
        and broken ground,
Down the hillside at a racing pace he went;
And he never drew the bridle till he landed safe and
        sound
At the bottom of that terrible descent.

He was right among the horses as they climbed the
  farther hill,
And the watchers on the mountain, standing mute,
Saw him ply the stockwhip fiercely; he was right among
  them still,
As he raced across the clearing in pursuit.
Then they lost him for a moment, where two mountain
  gullies met
In the ranges—but a final glimpse reveals
On a dim and distant hillside the wild horses racing yet,
With the man from Snowy River at their heels.

And he ran them single-handed till their sides were
  white with foam;
He followed like a bloodhound on their track,
Till they halted, cowed and beaten; then he turned their
  heads for home,
And alone and unassisted brought them back.
But his hardy mountain pony he could scarcely raise a
  trot,
He was blood from hip to shoulder from the spur;
But his pluck was still undaunted, and his courage fiery
  hot,
For never yet was mountain horse a cur.

And down by Kosciusko, where the pine-clad ridges
  raise
Their torn and rugged battlements on high,
Where the air is clear as crystal, and the white stars fairly
  blaze
At midnight in the cold and frosty sky,

And where around the Overflow the reed-beds sweep
    and sway
To the breezes, and the rolling plains are wide,
The Man from Snowy River is a household word today,
And the stockmen tell the story of his ride.

A. B. "BANJO" PATERSON

KENTUCKY BELLE

Summer of 'sixty-three, sir, and Conrad was gone
    away—
Gone to the country town, sir, to sell our first load of
    hay.
We lived in the log house yonder, poor as ever you've
    seen;
Roschen there was a baby, and I was only nineteen.

Conrad, he took the oxen, but he left Kentucky Belle;
How much we thought of Kentuck, I couldn't begin to
    tell—
Came from the Bluegrass country; my father gave her to
    me
When I rode north with Conrad, away from the
    Tennessee.

Conrad lived in Ohio—a German he is, you know—
The house stood in broad cornfields, stretching on, row
    after row;
The old folks made me welcome; they were kind as kind
    could be;
But I kept longing, longing, for the hills of the
    Tennessee.

O, for a sight of water, the shadowed slope of a hill!
Clouds that hang on the summit, a wind that never is
    still!
But the level land went stretching away to meet the
    sky—
Never a rise from north to south, to rest the weary eye!

From east to west, no river to shine out under the moon,
Nothing to make a shadow in the yellow afternoon;
Only the breathless sunshine, as I looked out, all forlorn,
Only the "rustle, rustle," as I walked among the corn.

When I fell sick with pining we didn't wait any more,
But moved away from the cornlands out to this river
    shore—
The Tuscarawas it's called, sir—off there's a hill, you
    see—
And now I've grown to like it next best to the Tennessee.

I was at work that morning. Someone came riding like
    mad
Over the bridge and up the road—Farmer Rouf's little
    lad.

Bareback he rode; he had no hat; he hardly stopped to
    say,
"Morgan's men are coming, Frau, they're galloping on
    this way.

"I'm sent to warn the neighbors. He isn't a mile behind;
He sweeps up all the horses—every horse that he can
    find;
Morgan, Morgan the raider, and Morgan's terrible men,
With bowie knives and pistols, are galloping up the
    glen."

The lad rode down the valley, and I stood still at the
    door—
The baby laughed and prattled, playing with spools on
    the floor;
Kentuck was out in the pasture; Conrad, my man, was
    gone;
Near, near Morgan's men were galloping, galloping on!

Sudden I picked up baby and ran to the pasture bar:
"Kentuck!" I called; "Kentucky!" She knew me ever so
    far!
I led her down the gully that turns off there to the right,
And tied her to the bushes; her head was just out of
    sight.

As I ran back to the log house at once there came a
    sound—
The ring of hoofs, galloping hoofs, trembling over the
    ground,

Coming into the turnpike out from the White-Woman
   Glen—
Morgan, Morgan the raider, and Morgan's terrible men.

As near they drew and nearer my heart beat fast in
   alarm;
But still I stood in the doorway, with baby on my arm.
They came; they passed; with spur and whip in haste
   they sped along;
Morgan, Morgan the raider, and his band six hundred
   strong.

Weary they looked and jaded, riding through night and
   through day;
Pushing on east to the river, many long miles away,
To the border strip where Virginia runs up into the west,
And for the Upper Ohio before they could stop to rest.

On like the wind they hurried, and Morgan rode in
   advance;
Bright were his eyes like live coals, as he gave me a
   sideways glance;
And I was just breathing freely, after my choking pain,
When the last one of the troopers suddenly drew his
   rein.

Frightened I was to death, sir; I scarce dared look in his
   face,
As he asked for a drink of water and glanced around the
   place;
I gave him a cup, and he smiled—'twas only a boy, you
   see,

Faint and worn, with dim blue eyes; and he'd sailed on
       the Tennessee.

Only sixteen he was, sir—a fond mother's only son—
Off and away with Morgan before his life had begun!
The damp drops stood on his temples; drawn was the
       boyish mouth;
And I thought me of the mother waiting down in the
       South!

O, plucky was he to the backbone and clear grit through
       and through;
Boasted and bragged like a trooper; but the big words
       wouldn't do;
The boy was dying, sir, dying, as plain as plain could
       be,
Worn out by his ride with Morgan up from the
       Tennessee.

But, when I told the laddie that I too was from the South,
Water came in his dim eyes and quivers around his
       mouth.
"Do you know the Bluegrass country?" he wistful began
       to say,
Then swayed like a willow sapling and fainted dead
       away.

I had him into the log house, and worked and brought
       him to;
I fed him and coaxed him, as I thought his mother'd do;
And, when the lad got better, and the noise in his head
       was gone,
Morgan's men were miles away, galloping, galloping on.

"O, I must go," he muttered; "I must be up and away!
Morgan, Morgan is waiting for me! O, what will Morgan
    say?"
But I heard a sound of tramping and kept him back from
    the door—
The ringing sound of horses' hoofs that I had heard
    before.

And on, on came the soldiers—the Michigan cavalry—
And fast they rode, and black they looked galloping
    rapidly;
They had followed hard on Morgan's track; they had
    followed day and night;
But of Morgan and Morgan's raiders they had never
    caught a sight.

And rich Ohio sat startled through all those summer
    days,
For strange, wild men were galloping over her broad
    highways;
Now here, now there, now seen, now gone, now north,
    now east, now west,
Through river valleys and cornland farms, sweeping
    away her best.

A bold ride and a long ride! But they were taken at last.
They almost reached the river by galloping hard and fast;
But the boys in blue were upon them ere ever they
    gained the ford,
And Morgan, Morgan the raider, laid down his terrible
    sword.

Well, I kept the boy till evening—kept him against his
    will—
But he was too weak to follow, and sat there pale and
    still;
When it was cool and dusky—you'll wonder to hear me
    tell—
But I stole down to that gully and brought up Kentucky
    Belle.

I kissed the star on her forehead—my pretty, gentle
    lass—
But I knew that she'd be happy back in the old
    Bluegrass;
A suit of clothes of Conrad's, with all the money I had,
And Kentuck, pretty Kentuck, I gave to the worn-out
    lad.

I guided him to the southward as well as I knew how;
The boy rode off with many thanks, and many a
    backward bow,
And then the glow it faded, and my heart began to swell,
As down the glen away she went, my lost Kentucky
    Belle!

When Conrad came in the evening the moon was
    shining high;
Baby and I were both crying—I couldn't tell him why—
But a battered suit of rebel gray was hanging on the wall,
And a thin old horse with drooping head stood in
    Kentucky's stall.

Well, he was kind, and never once said a hard word to
      me;
He knew I couldn't help it—'twas all for the Tennessee;
But, after the war was over, just think what came to
      pass—
A letter, sir; and the two were safe back in the old
      Bluegrass.

The lad had got across the border, riding Kentucky Belle;
And Kentuck she was thriving, and fat, and hearty, and
      well;
He cared for her, and kept her, nor touched her with
      whip or spur:
Ah! we've had many horses, but never a horse like her!

CONSTANCE FENIMORE WOOLSON

Riders

MOON LIGHT

Moon light
ribs the trail,
slashes the sweated
black-neck of my horse;
he, with eyes soft in half-sleep,
hurtles the torn thunder-dead trees
and gutted gulleys of April.
He, with hoofs high,
flings the dirt as we go,
flails the clouds of lilac smell
with purple-trailing tail,
laughs in his throat
across the banks of
spattered sand,
and in high fever—we
lean forward to leap the river
on the way
to May.

FREYA MANFRED

HAIKU, FOR CINNAMON

Rainy mid-morning,
You whinny waiting for our
Play-work together.

Where the sun touches,
You are burnished gold, stretching
To be assayed.

Ultra-butterball
Nuzzling me with warm, moist love,
I speak pats to you.

Up and down the lane,
Across the meadows, we are one
Graceful movement.

LILLIE D. CHAFFIN

GALLOPING

The rushing, the brushing, the wind in your face
The thudding of hooves and the quickening of pace
Not so clear is your gaze, blocked and dulled by a haze
You feel the horse in a kind of a daze.

You are numb to the feel of the ups and downs
The twists and turns, the curves and the rounds
You feel only the thud of the galloping hooves
And the regular jolt of the horse as he moves.

CORDELIA CHITTY (age 11)

HORSE

A
quarter horse, no rider
canters through the pasture

thistles raise soft purple burrs
her flanks are shiny in the sun
I whistle and she runs
almost sideways toward me

the oats in my hand are sweets to her:

dun mane furling in its breeze,
her neck
corseted with muscle,
wet teeth friendly against my hand—
how can I believe
you ran under a low maple limb
to knock me off?

JIM HARRISON

TO A HORSE

Now when we leave the windows of hay
behind us and canter over the clouds
below and chanting my words mount and whinny
like magic, I'm happy, I'm happy,
sweet mare: I never forget your name.

JILL HOFFMAN

THE FIELD

Somewhere in the field
we have broken open a hornet's nest.
A cloud of them rises from the earth,
anger growing darker.
I feel the horse tighten
and step crabwise. Her summer
coat has mellowed from its sheen
to a thick mat. She knows the carcass,
a dead deer the hunter never found
tangled in barbed wire at the woods' edge:
She panics and won't go near.
A cold wind springs like a whip
and snaps leaves off
and she leaps in fear.

Growing islands of lather
whiten her thoroughbred's coat
and her white breath clouds
the field which is growing smaller
smaller.

DOUGLAS LAWDER

THE GENTLED BEAST

At the kiss of my heel,
at the flex of my wrists,
he rears, resists
the signs of my will.

He balks, he tugs the rein,
dances to throw me.
I master him. He must show me
the size of his disdain.

In fugue of flesh and mind
we fight, and are conjoint:
hard counterpoint
contending to one end.

He must yield. When my finger
feels a mouth of feather,

and my boot's leather
bears on his flank no stronger

than a windblown seed,
only then shall he race
reinless, at his own pace:
a speed beyond my speed.

DILYS LAING

HOSSOLALIA

Bucephalus is neighing me a love song.
The tune is public domain, but the lyric
is pure hossolalia. He repeats
the chorus, whinneying and nickering
the wheedling notes over and over:
come   dear one   let us go   cantering
Bucephalus could go cantering alone
but he feels incomplete without me
on his back, so he stands at the fence
and thinks it to me in horsemusic.

Strummed by his song, I race past the stable,
mount bareback and cling to his mane.
We're off—off completely! Sunstruck, moonmad,
riding at noon without bridle or saddle,

in total communion.
He can read my mind
through my knees and heels.

MILDRED LUTON

ONCE UPON A NAG

Century Farms
rents horses by the hour.
Mine with eyes half hidden
under blue milk film
swivels an ear
and quivers a flank
to pester her flies.
Foot chest high
I lunge at the stirrup
land behind the pommel
hands to horn.
A hump in the saddle
a cluck of the tongue
and she clobbles on our way.

The groom guaranteed a lively ride
why this crippled pace?
Twenty-five minutes
not a trot

not a canter
will somebody wake her?
We round a bend
she blows a wet-jeweled snort
and leans toward home . . .
am I riding her or is she riding me?
Time to aim my heels at her seat!

MICHAEL BEIRNE McMAHON

RIDERS

At four p.m. small fingers moved the dial to one-six-"O"
And crackling radio gave out its daily episode.
Each afternoon a new group rode the airways—
Lone Ranger first, with Tonto, then Roy, Dale and
    Trigger,
Gene Autry and his old Chuck Wagon Gang,
Wild Bill and his falsetto side-kick Jingles
(With Sugar Crisps always shot straight from guns).
But Fridays were the best of all
For Bobby Benson's haunting call of "B-Bar-B"
Could transform me into a fearless wonder just his size.
When half an hour of thundering hooves
And blazing guns had died, I'd make my way outside,
As if by chance, mount dead pecan tree's lowest branch,
And ride its roughness saddle smooth—

Slight, twilight figure, flying free,
Across the phantom acres of the B-Bar-B.

LINDA PEAVY

THE GREY HORSE

A dappled horse stood at the edge of the meadow,
He was peaceful and quiet and grey as a shadow.
Something he seemed to be saying to me,
As he stood in the shade of the chestnut tree.

'It's a wonderful morning,' he seemed to say,
'So jump on my back, and let's be away!
It's over the hedge we'll leap and fly,
And up the hill to the edge of the sky.

'For over the hill there are fields without end;
On the galloping downs we can run like the wind.
Down pathways we'll canter, by streams we'll stray,
Oh, jump on my back and let's be away!'

As I went by the meadow one fine summer morn,
The grey horse had gone like a ghost with the dawn;
He had gone like a ghost and not waited for me,
And it's over the hilltop he'd surely be.

JAMES REEVES

BILLY COULD RIDE

I

Billy was born for a horse's back!—
That's what Grandfather used to say:—
He'd seen him in dresses, a-many a day,
On a two-year-old, in the old barn-lot,
Prancing around, with the bridle slack,
An his two little sunburnt legs outshot
So straight from the saddle-seat you'd swear
A spirit-level had plumbed him there!
And all the neighbors that passed the place
Would just haul up in the road and stare
To see the little chap's father boost
The boy up there on his favorite roost,
To canter off, with a laughing face.—
Put him up there, he was satisfied—
And O the way that Billy could ride!

II

At celebration or barbecue—
And Billy, a boy of fifteen years—
Couldn't he cut his didoes there?—
What else would you expect him to,
On his little mettlesome chestnut mare,
With her slender neck, and her pointed ears,
And the four little devilish hooves of hers?
The "delegation" moved too slow
For the time that Billy wanted to go!
And to see him dashing out of the line

At the edge of the road and down the side
Of the long procession, all laws defied,
And the fife and drums, was a sight divine
To the girls, in their white-and-spangled pride,
Wearily waving their scarfs about
In the great "Big Wagon," all gilt without
And jolt within, as they lumbered on
Into the town where Billy had gone
An hour ahead, like a knightly guide—
O but the way that Billy could ride!

III

"Billy can ride! Oh, Billy can ride!
But what on earth can he do beside?"
That's what the farmers used to say,
As time went by a year at a stride,
And Billy was twenty if he was a day!
And many a wise old father's foot
Was put right down where it should be put,
While many a dutiful daughter sighed
In vain for one more glorious ride
With the gallant Billy, who none the less
Smiled at the old man's selfishness
And kissed his daughter, and rode away,—
Touched his horse in the flank—and *zipp!*—
Talk about horses and horsemanship!—
Folks stared after him just wild-eyed. . . .
Oomh! the way that Billy could ride!

JAMES WHITCOMB RILEY

WINDY NIGHTS

Whenever the moon and stars are set,
    Whenever the wind is high,
All night long in the dark and wet,
    A man goes riding by.
Late in the night when the fires are out,
Why does he gallop and gallop about?

Whenever the trees are crying aloud,
    And ships are tossed at sea,
By, on the highway, low and loud,
    By at the gallop goes he.
By at the gallop he goes, and then
By he comes back at the gallop again.

ROBERT LOUIS STEVENSON

RIDING A ONE-EYED HORSE

One side of his world is always missing.
You may give it a casual wave of the hand
or rub it with your shoulder as you pass,
but nothing on his blind side ever happens.

Hundreds of trees slip past him into darkness,
drifting into a hollow hemisphere

whose sounds you will have to try to explain.
Your legs will tell him not to be afraid

if you learn never to lie. Do not forget
to turn his head and let what comes come seen:
he will jump the fences he has to if you swing
toward them from side that he can see

and hold his good eye straight. The heavy dark
will stay beside you always; let him learn
to lean against it. It will steady him
and see you safely through diminished fields.

HENRY TAYLOR

GIRLS ON SADDLELESS HORSES

Girls on saddleless horses
and wool scarving their cheeks
defy the glazed streets,
the wealthy heat of their bodies
(calyxed in sweaters and jackets)
thrives up from their horses
like forked slips and graftings,
the incontinent sap of their breaths
pokes stalks through the air—
such crunch and alarum of ice!

and under cramped elms
what a procession of greenery.

R. G. VLIET

ON THE FARM

Coming over the rise, passing
through fields planted
straight and perfect as graph-
paper, we turn at the trot

into a wood to come upon
the huge, shipwrecked bodies
of cars and trucks,
windowless, their unblinking

eyes reflecting nothing.
Everything reusable is
long gone. Here at the edge
of cornfields, the flotsam

of Fords and Chevys
flakes under the sun. Our horses
quiver past these doorless wonders
arching their necks

and blowing air through
their noses as if
in an instant all the junk
will burst into a flame.

BARBARA WINDER

DEXTER

Galloping away to the farthest pasture
Is black Dexter with the tangled mane.
Once he was part of a dream. He turned
When I whistled and trotted slowly to me.

But the day we were a mile from the farm,
He bolted and ran with me.
Rocking away as Dexter galloped
I felt he would never stop.

His chunky white teeth were tight on the bit.
His bunching muscles had a sound of their own
And leather scrubbed against leather.
The smell of sweat and fermented grain

Was on me and in the air.
Finally, he tired and gave me control,

Slowed to a walk, his sides were heaving.
Spittle flew as he shook his head.

When we reached the barn I was shaking.
Someone took the reins and helped me down.
I stood as the horse was walked to his stall
And I never went near him again.

Some nights the black horse comes into the dream
And like Black Beauty neighs his lonesomeness
For the child to come and ride.

JOAN BYERS GRAYSTON

THE BAD RIDER

I had a little pony,
    His name was Dapple Gray;
I lent him to a lady
    To ride a mile away.
She whipped him, she slashed him,
    She rode him through the mire;
I would not lend my pony now,
    For all the lady's hire.

(ENGLISH NURSERY RHYME)

ON DRESSING TO GO HUNTING

Some people stop hunting because they get tired,
Or they think they're too old, or their nerve has expired.
But when I give it up I will hazard a guess
It will be in connection with matters of dress.
The worst thing about hunting, to me, without doubt,
Is the business of dressing myself to go out.
It takes patience, and strength, and a great deal of time,
And before I have finished, I'll have run out of rhyme.

First I drag on a corset to hold up my back,
Which, without its support, might collapse with a crack.
Then I cover my top with a thick woollen vest,
While ankle length pants protect most of the rest.
Next I haul up my breeches to find myself faced
With the problem of how I shall fasten the waist.
I pull it together, but I never can quite
Do up the top buttons, for alas! it's too tight.
Still somehow I fix it by dint of brute force,
Praying nothing will burst till I'm safe on my horse.

To deal with my boots I depend on. French Chalk.
Once they're on, they're so snug I can only just walk.
And now is the time when the telephone bell
Rings out its shrill summons (to what? who can tell?).
I put down the pull-ons and hop to the 'phone,
But I'm always too late and the caller has gone.
So I fasten my bootstraps and straighten my back,
And proceed with the job of the rest of the tack.

If the stock is to fold, as it should, and look right,
It has to begin, round my neck, far too tight,
And I must endure the occasional pin,
Exceeding its duties and piercing my skin.
With numerous grips I then master my hair,
Which I push in a net too coarse-textured to tear,
And crowning this horrid arrangement I pop
A black velvet hunting cap slap on the top.
My coat and my waistcoat are threadbare and old,
But they keep the warmth in, and they keep out the cold.
Last the gloves, and the spurs, and the whip, and it's
    done,
With some cash in my pocket to pay for the fun.

And now comes the black moment when hobbling forth
I'm hit by the sting of the wind from the North,
Or a downpour of rain, with a promise of snow,
Till I ask myself, why in the world do I go?
To get soaking, and frozen, and frightened as well,
It's supposed to be pleasure, yet so often, it's Hell!

But at last breaks the day when the cold wind has
    dropped,
When the dark clouds have lifted, the downpour has
    stopped,
When the fences look black, when the soft sky is grey,
And without any doubt it's a real scenting day.
Quick then, bring me my breeches, my boots and the
    rest,
My pants, and my shirt, and my stock, and my vest.

Dressing may be a nightmare I can only just bear,
But I'll keep up the struggle for as long I dare.

(BY "A GRANDMOTHER")

STALLION

A gigantic beauty of a stallion, fresh and responsive to
    my caresses,
Head high in the forehead, wide between the ears,
Limbs glossy and supple, tail dusting the ground,
Eyes full of sparkling wickedness, ears finely cut, flexibly
    moving.

His nostrils dilate as my heels embrace him,
His well-built limbs tremble with pleasure as we race
    around and return.
I but use you a minute, then I resign you, stallion.
Why do I need your paces when I myself out-gallop
    them?
Even as I stand or sit passing faster than you.

WALT WHITMAN

EVENING RIDE

Swift cries answering back
the soft threats of dusk
perch overhead on boughs where I can't see;
my own music
creaks from the loving saddle
under me.

JILL HOFFMAN

Stable,
Ring,
and Track

THE STABLE

On the threshold of the stable smelling
nothing but the square bales of hay and giant
oaks that swallow the white hawk evenings,
I duck under a curtain of flies and approach
the horses like hours standing hours in a row.

JILL HOFFMAN

Up the hill,
Hurry me not;
Down the hill,
Worry me not;
On the level,
Spare me not;
In the stable,
Forget me not.

(CHILDREN'S RHYME)

AMANDA IS SHOD

The way the cooked shoes sizzle
dropped in a pail of cold water
the way the coals in the portable forge
die out like hungry eyes
the way the nails go in aslant
each one the tip of a snake's tongue

and the look of the parings
after the farrier's knife
has sliced through.

I collect them
four marbled white C's
as refined as petrified wood
and dry them to circles of bone
and hang them away on my closet hook

lest anyone cast a spell on Amanda.

MAXINE KUMIN

MORE TO IT THAN RIDING

Sponge out nostrils—ugh!—and eyes,
    Well groom mane and tail;
Muddy hooves? That's no surprise—
    Fresh water in a pail.

Rub his loins and back and neck
    With hay, as you've been told;
Warm enough? You'd better check—
    Chafe ears if these are cold.

Look at shoes, and see the limbs
    Aren't swollen, hot, or gashed.
If he— (One of his whims)
    Watch out you don't get splashed!

(Stable's messy, like a bog)
    Work on with dandy-brush.
Pick his feet. Make sure the frog
    Is clean—no smell of thrush.

Wisp him; oil his hooves; and when
    That's finished (*if* you're able),
First pack him off to grass, and *then*
    Start mucking out the stable!

                    J. A. LINDON

THE PALOMINO STALLION

Though the barn is so warm
that the oats in his manger,
the straw in his bed
seem to give off smoke—

though the wind is so cold,
the snow in the pasture
so deep he'd fall down
and freeze in an hour—

the eleven-month-old
palomino stallion
has gone almost crazy
fighting and pleading
to be let out.

ALDEN NOWLAN

THE RIDING STABLE IN WINTER

Here in the dim and the almost dark and the warmth of
    the truth
In this winter stable the Teacher says a few words and
    supernatural horses

Carry children. The little boys and girls high on their
   splendid natural horses
Like birds on a tree or stars in God's thought hold
   themselves in the powerful place
And poise themselves with pride and grace. They circle.
   The horses walk.
They trot. The children like fish in the dim and gorgeous
   sea in winter or summer
Go up and down or lovers in the vague but calling bed of
   the universe.
The Teacher says a few words and the great horses ride
   like Kings.
I cannot remember the names of the gifts or the horses or
   the stars or Beauty
But in the winter the children like the calm and the
   radiant made me remember these words.

JOHN TAGLIABUE

FEBRUARY

The horse, head-swinging,
stolid in the snow-caught
field, his flanks snow-blanketed,
up to his hocks in frost-locked
weeds; he was the first to sense
the feed-cart coming, the first

to whinny low, and breaking
like a series of small waves,
he was the first and strongest in the barn
when he was stabled.

BARBARA WINDER

TWO AT SHOWTIME

Ears cocked wide
sun catching in the water
on his back,
the horse of a darkened color
stands in the leafdance
morning breeze
shaven and shorn
bathed and shed

by the girl with wet feet
arms, hands, and front
as she dreams open-eyed
of the ribbons
the judge's decisions
and horses, horses, horses . . .
How absentmindedly

she pets the wet neck
of her horse!

SUZANNE BRABANT

FAITH

FIRST PART

I had a donkey
Took it to a Show.
Would it trot when I asked?
Oh dear no!

Did the little perisher
Do it out of spite?
After all, it trotted
At *home* alright!

At Shows it went peculiar,
And wouldn't be led.
"What's wrong?" I hissed at it,
And it said:

"Pardon me! I thought
You thought I wouldn't

Then I felt peculiar
And found that I *couldn't!*

"Next time if I have
Your faith and trust
I will trot for you
Until I bust!"

SECOND PART

I took my donkey
To another Show,
Thinking and *believing*
It would go.

It went like a bomb!
Just as it should!
And why not, pray?—
When I *knew* that it would!

Gone were the doubts
And the moments of stress—
Would it trot past the Judge!
Yes, yes, YES!

Let all us Owners
Take a vow today
Not to cause our donkeys
To turn round and say

"Pardon me! I thought
You thought I wouldn't!"

Then I felt peculiar
And found that I *couldn't!*"

MARJORIE DUNKELS

PLINY JANE

Stretching her head toward the stars
and strutting like a majorette,
Pliny Jane
enters the arena
at the Tennessee Walking Horse Show,
sniffs haughtily at the cameras,
switches her tail at the judges,
and snorting her disdain for the blue ribbon,
proceeds daintily,
picking her way through a field
of imaginary violets.

MILDRED LUTON

HUNTER TRIALS

It's awf'lly bad luck on Diana,
    Her ponies have swallowed their bits;
She's fished down their throats with a spanner
    And frightened them all into fits.

So now she's attempting to borrow.
    Do lend her some bits, Mummy, *do;*
I'll lend her my own for to-morrow,
    But to-day I'll be wanting them too.

Just look at Prunella on Guzzle,
    The wizardest pony on earth;
Why doesn't she slacken his muzzle
    And tighten the breech in his girth?

I say, Mummy, there's Mrs. Geyser
    And doesn't she look pretty sick?
I bet it's because Mona Lisa
    Was hit on the hock with a brick.

Miss Blewitt says Monica threw it,
    But Monica says it was Joan,
And Joan's very thick with Miss Blewitt,
    So Monica's sulking alone.

And Margaret failed in her paces,
    Her withers got tied in a noose,
So her coronets caught in the traces
    And now all her fetlocks are loose.

Oh, it's me now. I'm terribly nervous.
  I wonder if Smudges will shy.
She's practically certain to swerve as
  Her Pelham is over one eye.

                *   *   *

Oh wasn't it naughty of Smudges?
  Oh, Mummy, I'm sick with disgust.
She threw me in front of the Judges,
  And my silly old collarbone's bust.

                          JOHN BETJEMAN

RIDE 'IM COWBOY

Ride 'im cowboy, ride 'im,
Spur 'im up the neck,
Give 'im his head an' let 'im pitch;
That's a buckin' horse, by heck.
Careful, don' lose your stirrups,
Keep your hands away from the horn,
Stay with 'im, stay with 'im, cowboy
You're a rider, as sure as you're born.

Ride 'im cowboy, ride 'im,
As long as the cinches hold,
You're the first guy that ever stayed there

Since the day that bronc was foaled.
Don't go to pullin' leather,
Ride 'im straight up like a man;
Stay with 'im, stay with 'im, cowboy.
You're a champion if you can.

Ride 'im cowboy, ride 'im,
He's a bunch-grass buckin' fool,
He could swap both ends on a dollar bill,
An' he grunts like an army mule.
Ain't he a holy terror?
I'll say that's a ride worthwhile;
Stay with 'im, stay with 'im cowboy.
Oh hell—he's throwed you a mile.

A. L. FREEBAIRN

BRONCO BUSTING, EVENT #1

The stall so tight he can't raise heels or knees
when the cowboy, coccyx to bareback, touches down

tender as a deerfly, forks him, gripping the rope-
handle over the withers, testing the cinch,

as if hired to lift a cumbersome piece of brown
luggage, while assistants perched on the rails arrange

the kicker, a foam rubber band around the narrowest,
most ticklish part of the loins, leaning full weight

on neck and rump to keep him throttled, this horse,
"Firecracker," jacked out of the box through the sprung

gate, in the same second raked both sides of the belly
by ratchets on booted heels, bursts into five-way

motion: bucks, pitches, swivels, humps, and twists,
an all-over-body-sneeze that must repeat

until the flapping bony lump attached to his spine is
          gone.
A horn squawks. From the dust gets up a buster named
          Tucson.

MAY SWENSON

PONY GIRL

She pops their flanks with a rawhide whip,
Old Bill, Sugar, Charlie Blue, and other
Aged Shetlands, swag-backed, tacky-tailed,
Setting them off to trot weedy rings
Weighted with misses, cowboys, babies balanced
In folds of fat, bug-eyed, wet-nosed,

Ignoring dung, mud, listing stalls,
Fanning flies from her face with seventeen braids
Cupped and curled like tentacles of an octopus hat,
As lithe bones in slick leather habit
Load, unload day to her own nasal harp,
"Take your ticket, take your ticket,
Pick your speed, pick your steed."

JANE P. MORELAND

TO A RACE HORSE AT ASCOT

Even as your progenitors ran
in Greek festival,
fled before chariot on Roman field,
you run today:
even as the eohippus,
small ungulate, no bigger than a fox,
dolichocephalic, with no collarbone,
raced on its middle fingernail
toward first dawn.
Never restyled,
the number of cylinders never stepped up,
fleet, beautiful, perfectly coordinated, you run.
African mount of Spanish blood,
Arabian steed in sheik's regalia,
Roman filly flying down Salisbury plain,

you race today. And kings come
in thousand horsepower Bentleys
to cheer.

JENNIE M. PALEN

A DAY AT THE RACES

There they were
coming around the far turn
with the one I bet on
dead last.
I staked everything I had
on Poetry,
but there she was
trailing Science & Technology,
with Making Money
far out front,
leading by 9 lengths.
I looked to see if the jockey
was holding Poetry back,
if he was waiting
for the last minute
stretch drive,
but, no,
Making Money
won going away;

Science & Technology
finished Place & Show.
Some horse called Education
pulled up lame
& had to be walked away.
But there was my horse,
taking her time,
lopping in dead last
as if she weren't costing
anybody anything.
A 3 year old claiming race
& I had all those losing tickets
on her. I tell you, though,
when the saddle's off her
& the bit out of her mouth,
when she's alone in a green field,
she runs & runs & runs.

LOUIS PHILLIPS

HORSES

The long whip lingers,
Toys with the sawdust:
The horses amble
On a disc of dreams.

The drumsticks flower
In pink percussion
To mix with the metal
Petals of brass.

The needle runs
In narrower circles;
The long whip leaps
And leads them inward.

Piebald horses
And ribald music
Circle around
A spangled lady.

LOUIS MacNEICE

THE HORSE SHOW AT MIDNIGHT

I. THE RIDER

Now, the showground is quiet.
The spectators all have departed.
Along the wall of the arena
The jumps are lying, collapsed.
The moon shines down on the grandstand
As I walk out across the ring
Alone, watching for what may not be here.

I take my place as a judge
In the center of the ring, waiting.
Asleep in their stables, the horses
Awaken to my thought-out call
And rise from the straw and walk
To the ring, silently and formally.
One after another they march
Around the ring, proudly, like men.
I stand on my toes and speak softly—
They all start to gallop at once
Noiselessly, weightlessly,
Their hoofs beating only within me.
Around the ring, faster and faster,
Their manes like flame in the moonlight,
They gallop in single file,
Halt as I think the command,
Then walk out of the ring
Into darkness, proudly and softly.
One horse only stays with me
Straining to hear a command
That I am unable to utter.
On a sign from someone unseen
The jumps rise up into place
By themselves, hugely and suddenly.
The horse kneels down on the grass
And rises up with a rider.
As I watch from my place as a judge
My heart and my bones leave my body
And are heart and bones of this rider.
As the horse flies over the fences
The horseman whose heart is the judge's
Makes no movement or sound,

But the horse knows what he must do
And he takes the fences one by one
Not touching the poles or the ground.
At the end of the course he halts
And the fences retreat to the ringside,
Then my horse and his rider are gone.
Alone in the grandstand's shadow
I call to him time after time
But only my bones fill my body.
The rider and horse do not answer.
I walk across to the gate
Looking back once more at the ring
Watching for sound or a movement
Left behind by one horse that I love.
The empty ring does not echo
And the horse has left no hoofprints.
In the moonlight, alone, I sink down
Kneeling in nothing but bones
And I call to my horse once again
But the ring and the grandstand are quiet.

II. THE HORSE

In the darkened stable I move in my sleep
And my hoof stirs the straw and wakes me.
I rise, breathing softly, inhaling
The moonlight outside like perfume,
Straining to hear the command
That moved my hoof in the straw.
In my huge, shining shape I stand
Listening, and I hear the calling again.
Through the locked door of my stall,

Obeying, I march to the show ring,
Beside horses I cannot see, but feel
As their hoofs shake the air around me.
I march to the sound of a heart
That beats somewhere just ahead of me.
In the ring I lead a parade
In a circle, galloping and galloping,
And I wait for a change in the heartbeat.
I halt, and the others march out,
And I sink to my knees on the grass
As a body gets up on my back
And the man in the ring disappears.
I rise to my feet once again
And look around me at fences
Which have sprung like trees from the ground.
My shape fills the air as I fly
Over boards, stone walls, and poles,
And the bones on my back do not move.
Still I move to the beat of a heart
That brought me out of the stable.
I stop when I clear the last fence,
And the bones dismount, and I march
From the ring to the sound of the heart.
Back in my stable I lie down
Wide-eyed, breathless and shining,
Still hearing within me the call
That brought me over the jumps.
This time I cannot obey:
This man is only partly a rider
And the rider in him is within me.
Helpless, grief-stricken, and alone,
He kneels out there in the moonlight

With only his bones for a body,
His heart singing deeply within
A shape that moves with new life.
I believe in the singing, and sleep.

HENRY TAYLOR

Horse
Laughs

THE MARE

Look at the mare of Farmer Giles!
She's brushing her hooves on the mat;

Look at the mare of Farmer Giles!
She's knocked on the door, rat-a-tat!

With a clack of her hoof and a wave of her head
She's tucked herself up in the four-poster bed,
And she's wearing the Farmer's hat!

HERBERT ASQUITH

THE TRAIL HORSE

"If I could get Yeats on a horse, I'd put a new rhythm into English poetry."
—Ezra Pound

Get on, expecting the worst—a mount like a statue
Or a bucking runaway.
If neither happens, if this bay mare holds still,
Then you're off
The ground, not touching the ground except through her
Four stilted corners
Which now plop up and down as carefully
In the mud by the road

As if those hoofprints behind her were permanent.
You're in the saddle
As she clip-clops up the path on a slack rein,
Her nose leading the way
Under the pine boughs switching like her tail.
Give in. Sit still.
It won't be hard to let her have her head:
It's hers by a neck;
She'll keep it against your geeing, hawing, or whoaing.
This one's been bred
To walk from daybreak to darkness in the mountains
Up trail or down
And will do it without you tomorrow. The apparatus
Cinching and bridling her,
The leather and metal restraints for a prisoner
Who *won't* be convenient,
Who *won't* do what she's told or listen to reason,
Are mostly for show:
For example, take this place you're passing now—
Tall stumps and boulders,
Thirty degrees of slope and a narrow trail—
A time for judgment,
A time for the nice control of cause and effect.
Do you see the flies
Clustered around her eyelids, nipping their salt?
Or the humming wasp
Tossed from her tail to her rump where it sinks in?
Suddenly swivelling
And sliding, jerking tight as a slipknot
And rearing out from under
Arched like a cow and a half humped over the moon,
She leaves you alone,

And you part company on the only terms
Possible: hers being yours—
No straddler of winged horses, no budding centaur,
But a man biting the dust.

DAVID WAGONER

LORD EPSOM

A Horse, Lord Epsom did bestride
With mastery and quiet pride.
He dug his spurs into its hide.
The Horse, discerning it was pricked,
Incontinently bucked and kicked,
A thing that no one could predict!

Lord Epsom clearly understood
The high-bred creature's nervous mood,
As only such a horseman could.
Dismounting, he was heard to say
That it was kinder to delay
His pleasure to a future day.

*   *   *

He had the Hunter led away.

HILAIRE BELLOC

WAR HORSES
A Clerihew

Horses
Are no longer used in the Armed Forces.
Instead, the cavalry ride tanks.
No thanks.

WILLIAM COLE

THE HUNTSMEN

Three jolly gentlemen,
   In coats of red,
Rode their horses
   Up to bed.

Three jolly gentlemen
   Snored till morn,
Their horses champing
   The golden corn.

Three jolly gentlemen,
   At break of day,
Came clitter-clatter down the stairs
   And galloped away.

WALTER DE LA MARE

ON REARS

The rumps of horses:
such gross
roundness, such burnished
complete compactness,
such fat
economy.

And such bisection:
the matched
curvatures, the immaculate
contours, even, oval,
twinned!

The deep cleavage!
Dark as velvet, clean
as gloves;
how publicly, properly
private.

And the perfect gold droppings.

The rump's motion:
such lively friction,
valved revolutions, contra-
puntal rhythms.
The original ball
bearings. Round

as wheels. Mammoth oranges
rolling together.

And then!

The TAIL!

MARY HEDIN

THE RACING-MAN

My gentle child, behold this horse—
A noble animal, of *course*,
   But not to be relied on;
I wish he would not stand and snort;
Oh, frankly, he is *not* the sort
   Your father cares to ride on.
His head is tossing up and down,
And he has frightened half the town
   By blowing in their faces,
And making gestures with his feet,
While now and then he stops to eat
   In inconvenient places.
He nearly murdered me today
By trotting in the wildest way
   Through half a mile of forest;
And now he treads upon the curb,

Consuming some attractive herb
    He borrowed from the florist.
I strike him roughly with my hand;
He does not seem to understand;
    He simply *won't* be bothered
To walk in peace, as I suggest,
A little way towards the West—
    He prances to the No'th'ard.
And yet, by popular repute,
He is a mild, well-mannered brute,
    And very well connected;
Alas! it is the painful fact
That horses hardly ever act
    As anyone expected.
Yet there are men prepared to place
A sum of money on a race
    In which a horse is running,
An animal as fierce as this,
As full of idle prejudice,
    And every bit as cunning;
And it is marvelous to me
That grown-up gentlemen can be
    So simple, so confiding;
I envy them, but, O my son,
I cannot think that they have done
    A great amount of riding.

A. P. HERBERT

HORSE-GIRL

Karen can canter, Karen can
Gallop and trot and walk;
Karen can whinny, Karen can
Neigh and talk horses' talk.

Karen can canter, Karen can
Change leads and pace and prance;
Karen can rear up, Karen can
Dance the way horses dance.

Karen can canter, Karen can
Run from her flowing mane;
Karen can stand still, Karen can
Pose like a weather vane.

HENRY PETROSKI

TALLYHO-HUM

Have you ever gone visiting for a weekend of ravelry
Only to find yourself surrounded by the Cavalry?
Not regular cavalry like Hussars or Lancers or Northwest
    Mounted Police,
But people who actually ride horses for pleasure in times
    of peace.

People who expose themselves gratis to risks for which
　　we pay the Lancer, the Hussar and the Mountie,
People who recover from a broken rib at Meadowbrook
　　in time to fracture a vertebra at Peapack which will
　　just be knitting when they split a collarbone in
　　Harford County,
People who otherwise may be cynics and stoics,
But go yowling berserk whenever the cheerleader says
　　"Yoicks!"
Well, you can take the word of an old mossback
Who's never been on hossback,
It's very hard to chat
With people like that,
Because they are not very interested in talking about the
　　screen or the stage or the latest best-selling book or
　　dud book,
All they want to talk about is the Stud Book,
And willy nilly
You've got to hear about the children of the ch.f.,
And if you think you can safely join in a family
　　conversation, Dear me,
The mirth that you provoke when you ask after the
　　children of the b.g.
On such seas you are indeed a ship without a rudder
If like myself you do not know a hock from a girth or a
　　wither from an udder.
And you will feel about horses, even those born and
　　bred in Old Kentucky,
Much as you do about streptocucci.

OGDEN NASH

115

MINNIE MORSE

Of all the problems no one's solved
The worst is Minnie Morse's;
I mean why Minnie's so involved
With horses.

Since Minnie bought a horse this spring
(An animal named Mable)
She doesn't care to do a thing
But hang around the stable.

In school, she'll never ever pass.
She fills her notebook spaces
And messes up her books in class
By drawing horses' faces.
Last week our teacher, Miss McGrew,
Made Minnie stand—and said
She didn't mind a sketch or two
But now please write instead.
And Minnie sat again, and drew
Another horse's head.

"I said to *write*," cried Miss McGrew.
"Does someone have to force you?"
At which point, Minnie stomped her shoe
As if she wore a horseshoe,
And tossing back her mane of hair
While all the class just waited,
She said that horses didn't *care*
If girls got educated.

Well, if a horse is what you've got,
It's fine to want to please one;
But what I brood about a lot
Is Minnie acts like *she's* one.

In fact, the way she is today,
You can't get far with Minnie
Unless you live on oats and hay—
And whinny.

KAYE STARBIRD

SOME DAY

Some day I'll have a war horse
To ride me into battle,
Or maybe just a show horse
To prance and dance and daddle,
Or maybe just a cow horse
To help me herd my cattle,
Some day, some day, I'll have a horse;
Today I've got the saddle.

SHEL SILVERSTEIN

JACK AND HIS PONY, TOM

Jack had a little pony—Tom;
He frequently would take it from
The stable where it used to stand
and give it sugar with his hand.

he also gave it oats and hay
And carrots twenty times a day
And grass in basketfuls, and greens,
And swedes and mangolds, also beans,
And patent foods from various sources
And bread (which isn't good for horses)
And chocolate and apple-rings
And lots and lots of other things
The most of which do not agree
With Polo Ponies such as he.
And all in such a quantity
As ruined his digestion wholly
And turned him from a Ponopoly
—I mean a Polo Pony—into
A case that clearly must be seen to.

Because he swelled and swelled and swelled.
Which, when the kindly boy beheld,
He gave him medicine by the pail
And malted milk, and nutmeg ale,
And yet it only swelled the more
Until its stomach touched the floor.
And then it heaved and groaned as well
And staggered, till at last it fell

And found it could not rise again.
Jack wept and prayed—but all in vain.
The pony died, and as it died
Kicked him severely in his side.

Moral
Kindness to animals should be
Attuned to their brutality.

HILAIRE BELLOC

THE HORSE

Who is the noblest beast you can name?
The horse, of course.
Who loves to be saddled and thrills to be reined?
The horse, of course.
Who leads the parade to the blare of the band,
Who canters and trots at your slightest command,
Then relieves himself there right in front of the stand?
The horse, of course.

SHEL SILVERSTEIN

Workers,
Wild
Horses,
and War
Horses

HORSE GRAVEYARD

Some farms have graveyards tucked upon a knoll
under the shade of trees, maybe three slanting stones
and a patch or two of phlox or flowering spurge
holding their own for years against the grass.

There was none here. The older families had used
the village cemetery.

  But gradually the man
made one of his own. It was the horse graveyard.
Down under the foot of the pasture slope
they lay buried as carefully as any humans,
side by side, old black Tom and chestnut Jack,
Nancy Hanks in her time, and Dan the proud stepper.
The man nursed them all carefully until the end,
and when they grew beyond comfort to themselves
he led them down the pasture slope, he put a bullet
painlessly into their heads, he buried them
where they fell.

Now in a later day their bones
creep out like splinters of glass that have made the
      rounds
of a finger, white and light, the ponderous strength
of old Tom come to this, the froth a wave brings in.

And at one end is a granite boulder with no name,
laid by the man for Dan, best loved of his horses.

FRED LAPE

THE BARGE HORSE

The brasses jangle and the hausers tighten:
look how this huge-limbed beauty leans and strains
against the harness, that proud arch of neck
curved hard and low with labour, the round lines
all taut with tension. And the snub barge
wallowing after through the weeds and lilies
in the brown water of the long canal,
its broad beam heaving from the smoking shallows.

Haul, O haul, my lovely, lively horse.
Fire leaps from under the iron of your hoof,
your straight stiff foreleg tight with sinew now.
Even your masters, men, rehearse
this drag of labour on their own behalf,
their barges built from fear you never know.

SEÁN JENNETT

THE WAR HORSE

Then the Lord answered Job out of the whirlwind . . .
Do you give the horse his might?
    Do you clothe his neck with strength?
Do you make him leap like the locust?
    His majestic snorting is terrible.

124

He paws in the valley, and exults in his strength;
   he goes out to meet the weapons.
He laughs at fear, and is not dismayed;
   he does not turn back from the sword.
Upon him rattle the quiver,
   the flashing spear and the javelin.
With fierceness and rage he swallows the ground;
   he cannot stand still at the sound of the trumpet.
When the trumpet sounds, he says "Aha!"
   He smells the battle from afar,
   the thunder of the captains, and the shouting.

(THE BIBLE, REVISED STANDARD VERSION, JOB 39:19–25)

ALEXANDER TO HIS HORSE

Quiet, my horse, be quiet,
In the sunny meadow!
Shall your great heart riot
For terror of a shadow?

Oh, you are king of horses,
And king of men am I;
And we will take our courses
Together by-and-by.

We two will ride the meadows
Of all the world again—

We will not fight with shadows,
But men, my horse, with men!

ELEANOR FARJEON

THE STALLION

I am the only living thing
Who hates with lifted head,
With nostrils flared,
With rampant hooves.

I am the horse of war.
I am so dread
No man should dare
To mount my height.

Bellerophon rode me.
My jugular fed Genghis Khan.
I was by Alexander tamed.
I carried Die Valkyrie.

Who would saddle me
Had better walk instead
In his quiet garden.

BOYNTON MERRILL, JR.

FROM "VENUS AND ADONIS"

But lo, from forth a copse that neighbours by,
A breeding jennet, lusty, young and proud,
Adonis' trampling courser doth espy,
And forth she rushes, snorts and neighs aloud.
    The strong-necked steed, being tied unto a tree,
    Breaketh his rein and to her straight goes he.

Imperiously he leaps, he neighs, he bounds,
And now his woven girths he breaks asunder;
The bearing earth with his hard hoof he wounds,
Whose hollow womb resounds like heaven's thunder;
    The iron bit he crusheth 'tween his teeth,
    Controlling what he was controlled with.

His ears up-pricked; his braided hanging mane
Upon his compassed crest now stand on end;
His nostrils drink the air, and forth again,
As from a furnace, vapours doth he send;
    His eye, which scornfully glisters like fire,
    Shows his hot courage and his high desire.

Sometime he trots, as if he told the steps,
With gentle majesty and modest pride;
Anon he rears upright, curvets and leaps,
As who should say 'Lo, thus my strength is tried,
    And this I do to captivate the eye
    Of the fair breeder that is standing by.'

What recketh he his rider's angry stir,
His flattering 'Holla' or his 'Stand, I say'?

What cares he now for curb or pricking spur?
For rich caparisons or trappings gay?
    He sees his love, and nothing else he sees,
    For nothing else with his proud sight agrees.

Look when a painter would surpass the life
In limning out a well-proportionéd steed,
His art with nature's workmanship at strife,
As if the dead the living should exceed;
    So did this horse excel a common one
    In shape, in courage, colour, pace and bone.

Round-hoofed, short-jointed, fetlocks shag and long,
Broad breast, full eye, small head and nostril wide,
High crest, short ears, straight legs and passing strong,
Thin mane, thick tail, broad buttock, tender hide;
    Look what a horse should have he did not lack,
    Save a proud rider on so proud a back.

Sometime he scuds far off, and there he stares;
Anon he starts at stirring of a feather;
To bid the wind a base he now prepares,
And whe'er he run or fly they know not whether;
    For through his mane and tail the high wind sings,
    Fanning the hairs, who wave like feath'red wings.

He looks upon his love and neighs unto her;
She answers him as if she knew his mind;
Being proud, as females are, to see him woo her,
She puts on outward strangeness, seems unkind,
    Spurns at his love and scorns the heat he feels,
    Beating his kind embracements with her heels.

Then, like a melancholy malcontent,
He vails his tail, that, like a falling plume,
Cool shadow to his melting buttock lent;
He stamps, and bites the poor flies in his fume.
    His love, perceiving how he was enraged,
    Grew kinder, and his fury was assuaged.

THE PROBLEM OF WILD HORSES

"Many wild horses are small, scrawny, and often undernourished. . . . Yet, these wild horses are increasing at an astonishing rate."
                                                            —*Dr. Walt Conley*

Wild horses graze under a full moon
up country in Carson Forest.
Unlike tame horses who lie down
in stalls, they will sleep
all night under the stars,
tails giving an occasional
flip against flies.
It's good they don't know
how old they are, or that
winter is always coming, or
that somewhere there are bins
of grain and bales of hay.

Wild horses gallop on the dry
river-bed. Red flags quiver

in their nostrils when they run.
They don't know to be ashamed
of their washboard ribs.

At night if I close my eyes
tame mares and geldings go through
their paces shining and predictable.
So I lie with my eyes open, hoping
to see the watering-hole where
wild horses drink. If I am lucky,
some night I might even lie beside
them, sucking the good water
between my teeth.

BARBARA WINDER

UNSEEN HORSES

On a dark winter morning, I couldn't see
The horse but I heard him. His
Metal shoes scraping the ice covered
Ground. The clopping hooves slipping,

And the wheels of the milk wagon sliding,
In the slush of the salt melted ice.
The loaded wagon inched up Sixteenth
Street hill, over red bricks glazed with ice.

The horse's head was down, his withers clenched.
If he started slipping back, you had to set
The brake. Some drivers spoke to give their horses
Heart. Some, made dumb by the hate of their
      dependence,

Used a whip and were glad for the chance.
On top of the hill the route was level.
Up and down the alleys, the horse knew
The stops at the back sidewalks. On a dark

Winter afternoon, another horse I couldn't
See was the Lone Ranger's horse, Silver.
When the radio was on, I heard him gallop
In the living room. A sharp cloppity clop,

Cloppity clop, staccato as a machine gun.
Someone with a sense of rhythm
And a pair of wooden blocks, made a picture
Of a brave horse that could untie knots.

JOAN BYERS GRAYSTON

MONOLOGUE OF THE RATING MORGAN IN RUTHERFORD COUNTY

Star-face Lightfoot, sired by the Fox,
champed in his paddock, pawing rocks.

He neighed and swore: By God's fetlocks,
that a round-rumped stallion of my blood
be prostitute to a sign: At Stud!

How I could gallop into a battle,
or at the plow make the trace-chains rattle . . .
yet here I neighbour a flock of cattle.
My name is wind, my hoofs swift flame,
my eyes are lightning, my breath is foam—
my clientele is but *les femmes*.

When passing geldings and fillies neigh,
"Hi there, Dad!" that's not to say,
"Big Boy, that was a race today!"

It's merely a snicker, half inside,
as people give to a brand-new bride.
Lord, is there nothing left for a horse
but a daily quota of intercourse?

C. F. MacINTYRE

GOING TO TOWN

One of their horses was Nancy Hanks.
She came from the route of a city grocer.
She was old but lively. The woman drove her.
Often the boy and the woman went to town alone.

He liked the ride. His mother drove with both hands.
She leaned out awkwardly over the dashboard.
Excitement brought spots of red in her cheeks.
Nancy Hanks shook her head, she wanted to run,
her feet slap-slapped on the hard dirt road,
the dust rose behind the rattling wheels.

Coming home was slower. Nancy Hanks knew the way.
She walked up the hills, nobody had to drive her.
His mother rested the lines on her knees,
she talked of the future, the wheels ground on earth.
When they topped the last hill Nancy Hanks brightened,
food and stable called her, she started to trot.
The woman took the lines in both hands again.
The cool air of the hills rushed past their faces.
The boy liked coming home better than going.

FRED LAPE

At Pasture

FIVE HORSES

Midday, midsummer, the field is watercolor green.
In the center, slats of an open paddock frame.
A rusty bathtub for water trough in foreground shade.
Five horses—two brown, two pinto, one a buckskin
                                                —wade

          the wide green. They are made short by the stature
    of the grass—hoofs and half their muzzles unseen.
    They keep the composition balanced by their ease
    and placement. On a rectangle of sun, the two brown
    backs, like polished tables, solid, reddish rove.

        The black-on-whites, turned hinders to the wood,
          necks down, feel a slow breeze drag the scarves
        of their manes aslant. One's whole head is a dark
                                                    hood
            through which the ears, unpainted, point. The
                                    other's a mare
            with astonishing blue eyes, and all blond,
                                except for a pale

        tan patch over stifle and loin. The buckskin,
                                    youngest,
        crops in shade alone, tail thrown over tawny rump
    in a constant feathery rotor against flies.
    They move and munch so gradually, the scene
    seems not to change: clean colors outlines on mat-green,

under a horizontal wash of steady blue
that ink-sharp darker swallows, distant, dip into.
That pasture was the end of one of our walks.
We brought carrots that we broke and passed
on the flats of our hands, to the lips of Buck
and Blue,

to Spook, Brown I and Brown II, who nipped and
jostled
each other over the gate to get them.
They'd wait while we stroked their forelocks and
smooth jaws.
I could look into the square pupils of the palfrey, Blue,
her underlip and nostrils, like a rabbit's, pink.

Pied spots, as on a cheetah, showed faint under the
hair
of Buck, your horse: you liked him best.
Close up, we rubbed the ragged streaks and stars
on their
foreheads and chests, slapped their muscular
necks,
while they nudged us, snuffling our
pockets for more.

Now we've gone past summer and the green field,
but I could draw
their profiles, so distinguished the five faces stay in
view,

leaning over the gate boards toward our coming,
waiting for carrots, staring, yearning in a row.

MAY SWENSON

A MARE

Lovely Fia was the summer queen
And the sun-bodied light of winter: she so slender
Of pastern, fine of cannon, sloped in the shoulders
To all perfection, with that gazelle head set
Arched beneath the drawn bow of her neck;
She who rose blazing from the dusky stall
And lunged on the snaffle, who reared on high white
    stockings,
Light-mouthed, light-footed, blasting her loud whinny,
Saying among the oak trees, "Ha ha!" She was a mirror
Of flame, and when she ran, then she ran burning,
Swift as the falcon that stoops through the windless sky.

Fiamma, who can tell of all your richness?
You were a dragon horde, gold-red and willful.
How dark the winter rains are falling now!
I cannot find your peer in any pasture.

KATE BARNES

MORGANS IN OCTOBER

Skittery two-year-olds
bounding down a pebbled slope
dodge tatterdemalion oaks—and then
caper and shy, toss thick manes
and dazzle-eye.

Snorting, they rocket
and race with the wind, then they
halt, pirouette and race off again;
out of sight, all that's left is
a clatter of leaves.

SUZANNE BRABANT

THE RUNAWAY

Once when the snow of the year was beginning to fall,
We stopped by a mountain pasture to say, "Whose colt?"
A little Morgan had one forefoot on the wall,
The other curled at his breast. He dipped his head
And snorted at us. And then he had to bolt.
We heard the miniature thunder where he fled,
And we saw him, or thought we saw him, dim and gray,
Like a shadow against the curtain of falling flakes.

"I think the little fellow's afraid of the snow.
He isn't winter-broken. It isn't play
With the little fellow at all. He's running away.
I doubt if even his mother could tell him, 'Sakes,
It's only weather.' He'd think she didn't know!
Where is his mother? He can't be out alone."
And now he comes again with clatter of stone,
And mounts the wall again with whited eyes
And all his tail that isn't hair up straight.
He shudders his coat as if to throw off flies.
"Whoever it is that leaves him out so late,
When other creatures have gone to stall and bin,
Ought to be told to come and take him in."

ROBERT FROST

CATCHING A HORSE

When you get out there
holding the rope and the halter
and the carrots
as casually as you can,
remember that she'll
outrun you at a trot,
so don't rush right up
to her silk flanks

and expect her
to turn and slip
her head into the leather.

Instead, she'll flash
her eyes, swing her
head around in a split-
second, and disappear
over the ridge
flinging clots of
mud back at you.

But offer her the carrots
as if that's why you
trudged all the way
out there in the rain
with the wind beating
your coat against
your legs. Then
while she's munching
on the second, move your arm
slowly to encircle her
neck as if you were
giving her a hug. Before
she draws back

put the rope around
her with your other
hand and get ready
for her to back up,
ears flat and nostrils

quivering. Then give her
another carrot and slip
the halter over her nose
while she's still chewing,
clipping the rope
under her chin so you
won't have to dig in
with your heels or start
all over again in another
part of the pasture.

Now start whistling
and lead her into
the barn.

BARBARA WINDER

THE HORSES

I climbed through woods in the hour-before-dawn dark.
Evil air, a frost-making stillness,

Not a leaf, not a bird—
A world cast in frost. I came out above the wood

Where my breath left tortuous statues in the iron light.
But the valleys were draining the darkness

Till the moorline—blackening dregs of the brightening
      grey—
Halved the sky ahead. And I saw the horses:

Huge in the dense grey—ten together—
Megalith-still. They breathed, making no move,

With draped manes and tilted hind-hooves,
Making no sound.

I passed: not one snorted or jerked its head.
Grey silent fragments

Of a grey silent world.

I listened in emptiness on the moor-ridge.
The curlew's tear turned its edge on the silence.

Slowly detail leafed from the darkness. Then the sun
Orange, red, red erupted

Silently, and splitting to its core tore and flung cloud,
Shook the gulf open, showed blue,

And the big planets hanging—
I turned

Stumbling in the fever of a dream, down towards
The dark woods, from the kindling tops.

And came to the horses.
There, still they stood,
But now steaming and glistening under the flow of light,

Their draped stone manes, their tilted hind-hooves
Stirring under a thaw while all around them

The frost showed its fires. But still they made no sound.
Not one snorted or stamped,

Their hung heads patient as the horizons,
High over valleys, in the red levelling rays—

In din of the crowded streets, going among the years, the
faces,
May I still meet my memory in so lonely a place

Between the streams and the red clouds, hearing
curlews,
Hearing the horizons endure.

TED HUGHES

WISDOM

Knee-deep in coldness, muzzle buried white,
The pony nuzzles for the grass
Last night's fierce blizzard buried out of sight.
The Appaloosa's frecks are all that show
Where she begins and ends against a snow
The color of her lightness. I watch both
Horses pawing drifts, hooves digging deep,
Breaking the barren whiteness, making trails
Along the fence row. When this fails
To yield enough, the two will spurn
Such efforts primitive and turn
To man for hay thrown from the stack
Piled in the shed. Whoever said
That animals are wise enough to forage
For themselves has said a truth—
But only if they lack the chance
To forage otherwise—
An equal wisdom, I'd surmise.

LINDA PEAVY

THE STALLION

The grey grass in the early winter
Stiffens and crinkles up for cold;

The air withers the big hemlocks
And bracken fronds are brown and old.

"Where is the world?" said the black stallion:
And shook his head: and stamped in wonder:
"Where is the world? I smell battle,
I hear shouting and hooves' thunder."

Over the frozen field he clatters
To reach the time his bones remember.
Poor stallion! There's nothing here
But a bare hedge and bleak December.

ALAN PORTER

GOING AWAY

The horses are going away
The tall mare and the four-year-old.
Their bridles lie by the drive,
And their gear and what is left of the oats.

They do not know. They are out there sleeping.
Over them the tin roof bangs in the wind.

They will wade into acres of grass
And hear the new sound of a sea

That breaks past the hill and the steady branches of oaks
In a place where the roads have not come yet.

How they will run in the big pasture
Or stand, flicking their tails in the sunlight
Those high beasts that looked over our shoulders
Or stood silent, nuzzling, blocking the way.

They called to us when we were slow at evening.
The young one was born here.

We will go back into our houses
We will forget how large the world was once.

ANN STANFORD

ORCHARD

The mare roamed soft about the slope,
Her rump was like a dancing girl's.
Gentle beneath the apple trees
She pulled the grass and shook the flies.
Her forelocks hung in tawny curls;
She had a woman's limpid eyes,
A woman's patient stare that grieves.
And when she moved among the trees,

The dappled trees, her look was shy,
She hid her nakedness in leaves.
A delicate though weighted dance
She stepped while flocks of finches flew
From tree to tree and shot the leaves
With songs of golden twittering;
How admirable her tender stance.
And then the apple trees were new,
And she was new, and we were new,
And in the barns the stallions stamped
And shook the hills with trumpeting.

RUTH STONE

MARE

When the mare shows you
her yellow teeth, stuck
with clover and gnawed leaf,
you know they have combed
pastures of spiky grasses,
and tough thickets.

But when you offer her
a sweet, white lump
from the trembling plate

of your palm—she trots
to the gate, sniffs—
and takes it with velvet lips.

JUDITH THURMAN

Certain
Special
Horses

HORSES

Horses of earth
Horses of water
Great horses of grey cloud

A blizzard of horses

Dust
and the ponies of dust
Horses of muscle and blood

Chestnuts Roans Blacks
Palominos
Wild dapple of Appaloosas

Spanish ponies
cow-ponies
Broncs Mustangs
Arabians Morgans Tennessee Walkers
Trotters
Shetlands
Massive matched Percherons

Horses
and the names of horses
Whirlaway Man o' War Coaltown
Canonero
Foolish Pleasure

Horses with tails of smoke
The giddy laughter of horses

Horses of war
their necks clothed in thunder
nostrils wide

The ground beneath them
terrible to look on

Horses of anger
Horses of cruelty
wringing the iron bit in their mouths

The horses of Psyche

Blake's horses
The horses of instruction
Horses of breath

Dawn horses
And the one horse in the heart

that runs
and runs

ROBERT DANA

HORSE

Horse skin; hessian or hard hot silk.
Horse; muscle, packed round bone;
Horse's eye; large, dark, swivels in blue milk.

Alone, capricious he runs, making fire from stone
His hard feet built up with tuned steel.
But white wives in the village wait and pine

For men, who gripped beneath their groins, can feel
The striding muscle and the bending spine,
Riding, flank and mouth, the beauty beast.

His long face enters the wind. Veins river
The surface of his head; his powered neck creased
To tug of bit. Nerves, like tempered musical strings,
    quiver.

Distant, caught on the horizon, he glides sinuously,
    seeming
Less actual, more magical, as shadow horses in some
    awed dreaming.

GERARD BENSON

COMANCHE

The only member of General Custer's party to survive the Battle of Little Big Horn was
a horse named Comanche. He is stuffed and on display in a museum in Kansas.

They think I like it here, I guess,
stuffed and boxed in glass in Kansas
but I don't. I don't like being
saddled up and never watered, never fed
or let to rub against a tree. And I don't
like my ears pricked up by wires, man
there isn't anything to *hear*.

For almost fifteen years after Custer bit
the dust, I had a pleasant deal at Riley—
Got to walk around the Fort and jaw
with Korn the blacksmith, got my eats
and rubdowns, dropped my apples
where I pleased—and all I had to do
was lead the regiment in fancy marches

now and then, draped in mourning
—thanks to Col. Sturgis who had made a speech
concerning Bloody Tragedy and Special Pride
and Desperate Struggle. God and it was hot
and women cried, but anyway, because I didn't fall
at Little Big Horn, Sturgis gave this order:
no one rides or works me.

Fine. No more Keoghs kicking in my guts
("rugged" Capt. Myles Keogh owned and rode me),
no more massacres and thirsty drives—
just me and gentle Korn and swishing flies,

and eventually a decent death.
But look at me, I lived to thirty-one, a tasty age,
and then they shot me full of nothing.

GARY GILDNER

NAMES OF HORSES

All winter your brute shoulders strained against collars,
        padding
and steerhide over the ash hames, to haul
sledges of cordwood for drying through spring and
        summer,
for the Glenwood stove next winter, and for the
        simmering range.

In April you pulled cartloads of manure to spread on the
        fields,
dark manure of Holsteins, and knobs of your own
        clustered with oats.
All summer you mowed the grass in meadow and
        hayfield, the mowing
machine clacketing beside you, while the sun walked
        high in the morning,

and afternoon's heat, you pulled a clawed rake through
        the same acres,

gathering stacks, and dragged the wagon from stack to
    stack,
and the built hayrack back, up the hill to the chaffy barn,
three loads of hay a day, from standing grass in the
    morning.

Sundays you trotted the two miles to church, with the
    light load
of a leather top buggy, and grazed in the sound of
    hymns.
Generation on generation, your neck rubbed the
    windowsill
of the stall, smoothing the wood as the sea smooths
    glass.

When you were old and lame, when your shoulders hurt
    bending to
graze, one October the man who fed you and kept you,
    and harnessed you every
morning, led you through corn stubble to sandy ground
    above Eagle Pond
and dug a hole beside you where you stood shuddering
    in your skin,

and lay the shotgun's muzzle in the boneless hollow
    behind your ear,
and fired the slug into your brain, and felled you into
    your grave,
shoveling sand to cover you, setting goldenrod upright
    above you,
where by next summer a dent in the ground made your
    monument.

For a hundred and fifty years, in the pasture of dead
    horses,
roots of pine trees pushed through the pale curves of
    your ribs,
yellow blossoms flourished above you in autumn, and in
    winter
frost heaved your bones in the ground—old toilers, soil
    makers:

O Roger, Mackerel, Riley, Ned, Nellie, Chester, Lady
    Ghost.

DONALD HALL

NEVADA

Some cowpoke named her Nevada
the one maybe who caught her,
4-year-old bay
filly with little Arab ears
long mane which sprayed
black
in the boy's eyes
when he raced her
                wild mare, mustang

become a kid's horse: his mother
changed her name to Butterfly

Twice rearing she fell backwards with
him he slipped aside

In the hills
behind Napa
he stands by her as
she spooks, lunges free, stampedes
around the valley
stirrups flogging
mane ragged sky, leaping up outcroppings
plunging down, ripping through chaparral
wild
horse again
until she spins
races back down the valley's middle
ears flat to her head
straight at the boy standing numb
with surprise as she comes for him
nostrils big
eyes rolled, to
squat from a dead run, skidding up to him
halting
to stand there trembling, blowing, slobbering
the half-breed bit
nervously working the roller
with her tongue

slowly he reaches
grips the rein, leads her a pace
pulls the cinch

swings into the saddle
dogtrots out of that valley

                              forever

STANLEY NOYES

THE BLOOD HORSE

Gamorra is a dainty steed,
Strong, black, and of a noble breed,
Full of fire and full of bone,
With all his line of fathers known;
Fine his nose, his nostrils thin,
But blown abroad by the pride within!
His mane is like a river flowing,
And his eyes like embers glowing
In the darkness of the night,
And his pace as swift as light.

Look,—how round his straining throat
Grace and shifting beauty float;
Sinewy strength is in his reins,
And the red blood gallops through his veins:
Richer, redder, never ran
Through the boasting heart of man.
He can trace his lineage higher
Than the Bourbon dare aspire,—

Douglas, Guzman, or the Guelph,
Or O'Brien's blood itself!

He, who hath no peer, was born
Here, upon a red March morn.
But his famous fathers dead
Were Arabs all, and Arab-bred,
And the last of that great line
Trod like one of a race divine!
And yet,—he was but friend to one
Who fed him at the set of sun
By some lone fountain fringed with green;
With him, a roving Bedouin,
He lived (none else would he obey
Through all the hot Arabian day),
And died untamed upon the sands
Where Balkh amidst the desert stands.

BRYAN W. PROCTER (BARRY CORNWALL)

THE FOUR HORSES

White Rose is a quiet horse
    For a lady to ride,
Jog-trotting on the high road
    Or through the countryside.

Grey Wolf is a hunter
    All muscle and fire;
Day long he will gallop
    And not tumble or tire.

Black Magic's a race-horse;
    She is gone like a ghost,
With the wind in her mane
    To whirl past the post.

But munching his fill
    In a field of green clover
Stands Brownie the cart-horse,
    Whose labor is over.

JAMES REEVES

HORSE

His bridle hung around the post;
The sun and the leaves made spots come down;
I looked close at him through the fence;
The post was drab and he was brown.

His nose was long and hard and still,
And on his lip were specks like chalk.
But once he opened up his eyes,
And he began to talk.

He didn't talk out with his mouth;
He didn't talk with words or noise.
The talk was there along his nose;
It seemed and then it was.

He said the day was hot and slow,
And he said he didn't like the flies;
They made him have to shake his skin,
And they got drowned in his eyes.

He said that drab was just about
The same as brown, but he was not
A post, he said, to hold a fence.
"I'm horse," he said, "that's what!"

And then he shut his eyes again.
As still as they had been before.
He said for me to run along
And not to bother him any more.

ELIZABETH MADOX ROBERTS

CLANCY

We bought him at auction, tranquillized to a drooping
    halt,
A blue-roan burro to be ridden by infants in arms, by
    tyros

Or the feeblest ladies, to be slapped or curried or
    manhandled—
A burro for time exposures, an amiable lawnmower.

But he burst out of his delivery truck like a war-horse,
Figure-eighting all night at the end of his swivel chain,
Chin high, octuple-gaited, hee-hawing through two
    octaves
Across our field and orchard, over the road, over the
    river.

While I fenced-in our farm to keep him from
    barnstorming
Neighbors and dignified horses, then palisaded our
    house
Like a beleaguered fort, my wife with sugar and rolled
    oats
And mysteries of her own coaxed him slowly into her
    favor.

He stood through the muddiest weather, spurning all
    shelter,
Archenemy of gates and roofs, mangler of halters,
Detector of invisible hackamores, surefooted hoofer
Against the plots of strangers or dogs or the likes of me.

But she would brush him and whisper to him out of
    earshot
And feed him hazel branches and handfuls of
    blackberries
And run and prance beside him, while he goated and
    buck-jumped,

Then stood by the hour with his long soft chin on her
    shoulder

While I was left on the far side of my own fence
Under the apple trees, playing second pitchfork
Among a scattering of straw over the dark-gold burro-
    apples
Too powerful for any garden, even the Hesperides.

And I still watch from exile as, night or morning, they
    wander
Up slope and down without me, neither leading nor
    following
But simply taking their time over the important pasture,
Considering dew and cobwebs and alfalfa and each
    other.

And all his ancestors, once booted through mountain
    passes
Bearing their grubstaked packtrees, or flogged up dusty
    arroyos
To their bitter ends without water, are grazing now in
    the bottom
Of her mind and his, digesting this wild good fortune.

                                          DAVID WAGONER

WHITE HORSES

Count the white horses you meet on the way,
Count the white horses, child, day after day,
Keep a wish ready for wishing—if you
Wish on the ninth horse, your wish will come true.

I saw a white horse at the end of the lane,
I saw a white horse canter down by the shore,
I saw a white horse that was drawing a wain,
And one drinking out of a trough: that made four.

I saw a white horse gallop over the down,
I saw a white horse looking over a gate,
I saw a white horse on the way into town,
And one on the way coming back: that made eight.

But oh for the ninth one: where *he* tossed his mane,
And cantered and galloped and whinnied and swished
His silky white tail, I went looking in vain,
And the wish I had ready could never be wished.

Count the white horses you meet on the way,
Count the white horses, child, day after day,
Keep a wish ready for wishing—if you
Wish on the ninth horse, your wish will come true.

ELEANOR FARJEON

THE HORSE

I will not change my horse with any that treads . . .
When I bestride him, I soar, I am a hawk.
He trots the air; the earth sings when he touches it.
The basest horn of his hoof is more musical than the
      pipe of Hermes . . .
He's of the color of the nutmeg and of the heat of the
      ginger . . .
He is pure air and fire, and the dull elements
Of earth and water never appear in him,
But only in patient stillness while his rider mounts
      him . . .
It is the prince of palfreys. His neigh is like
The bidding of a monarch, and his countenance
Enforces homage.

WILLIAM SHAKESPEARE

(*from* King Henry V, *Act 3, Scene 6*)

THROWN AWAY

And some are sulky, while some will plunge.
(*So ho! Steady! Stand still, you!*)
Some you must gentle, and some you must lunge.
(*There! There! Who wants to kill you?*)

Some—there are losses in every trade—
Will break their hearts ere bitted and made,
Will fight like fiends as the rope cuts hard,
And die dumb-mad in the breaking-yard.

RUDYARD KIPLING

ON BUYING A HORSE

One white foot, try him;
Two white feet, buy him;
Three white feet, put him in the dray;
Four white feet, give him away;
Four white feet, and a white nose,
Take off his hide and feed him to the crows.

(TRADITIONAL)

GOLDEN GRAIN

Honey and Sherry and little Bashaw,
Waiting for me at the barnyard gate,

All the more loving, since dinner is late.
Honey and Sherry and little Bashaw.
These are my horses by love and by law.

Honey and Sherry and little Bashaw,
Up to their knees in the frozen grass.
The wind is metallic, icy and cold,
Their manes are copper, their coats are gold.
And the sun goes down like a gong of brass.
The grain in my hand, that I try to hold,

Streams through my fingers like years that pass,
Overflows like my heart, like the spring in the thaw,
Honey and Sherry and little Bashaw.

HELEN M. WRIGHT

Title Index

172

Author Index

First Line Index

177

178

179